T0164237

BLUE DAUGHTER OF THE RED SEA

Blue
Daughter
of the
Red Sea

A Memoir

METI BIRABIRO

The University of Wisconsin Press

Terrace Books

The University of Wisconsin Press
1930 Monroe Street
Madison, Wisconsin 53711

www.wisc.edu/wisconsinpress/

3 Henrietta Street
London WC2E 8LU, England

5   4   3   2   1

Printed in the United States of America

Library   of   Congress   Cataloging-in-
Publication Data
Birabiro, Meti.
Blue daughter of the Red Sea: a memoir /
Meti Birabiro.
p. cm.
ISBN 0-299-19570-8 (cloth: alk. paper)
1. Birabiro, Meti. 2. Ethiopian Americans—Biography. 3. Ethiopia—Biography. I. Title.
E184.E74B57 2004
305.892'8073'092—dc22
2003020577

Terrace Books, a division of the University of Wisconsin Press, takes its name from the Memo-
rial Union Terrace, located at the University of Wisconsin–Madison. Since its inception in
1907, the Wisconsin Union has provided a venue for students, faculty, staff, and alumni to
debate art, music, politics, and the issues of the day. It is a place where theater, music, drama,
dance, outdoor activities, and major speakers are made available to the campus and the community. To learn more about the Union, visit www.union.wisc.edu.

This book is dedicated to my one and only hero, my mother, Aklile, with all my love.

I have witnessed the affliction of my people . . .
and have heard their cry of complaint against their slave drivers,
so I know well what they are suffering.
Therefore I have come down to rescue them . . .
and lead them out of that land into a good and spacious land,
a land flowing with milk and honey . . .

Exodus 3:7–8

Table of Contents

Preface

EVERY SEASON IS A SEASON OF HARVEST. I gather all my equipments and set to work. I read to learn. I write to learn. I travel to learn. I socialize to learn. But I still have not learned to understand. This is how and why the project of writing a memoir started: I wanted to learn to understand. I began jotting down excerpts from the past. I made phone calls to distant lands. I visited the ghosts. I interviewed strangers. I talked to friends. I went to therapy. The people that I had considered dead in my heart came back to life. The umbilical cord that attached the past to the present, the mother to the child, the citizen to the gypsy, and the home to the strange land found its way to me. *Blue Daughter of the Red Sea* is not a complete book. It is a book of fragments. It is a book of revelation but it is also a book that has learned to silence. It is a book that has sat in the drawer for years before and after composition for fear of damaging repercussions. *Blue Daughter of the Red Sea* is the child of ambivalence, torn between two worlds. It is the child that knows silence but prefers to put its foot in its mouth. It is the child that leaves home to find home but gets lost in between. *It is the child that does not belong anywhere or to anyone. Blue Daughter of the Red Sea* is the story that finds voice in the embers of memory, in the face of melancholy and in the turbulent waters of solitude. Did I learn to understand? Maybe, only a little. However, the reader might not understand this book entirely. She and he will run into many holes that I did not fill, either for lack of memory or simply because I chose not to. I have ever been envious of people who tell their stories without reservations. Their pasts seem to flow as waterfalls that have beginnings and endings. My past is a mystery that lacks cardinal points. My past is also history that belongs to other people as much as it belongs to me. I have tried my best to protect myself, my angels, and my demons by disguising everyone under different names and in some cases continuing to keep our secrets as I'd always done. I hope you all enjoy the read; and whenever you stumble into a hole, use your imagination.

Acknowledgments
and Thanks

My God, You are my danseur noble in this complicated dance.
Mom, for the prayers and for restoring memory.
My Sister, for opening the door out of misery.
My Vale (*la mia amica dei sogni*), for your devoted friendship.
My Friends, from the beginning to the end, You are my support.
My Teachers, in all three continents, for flattering me.
Professore Petri, for providing the eye to see the potential when it was most needed.
Michael Ortiz, Tricia Brock, Jeri Famighetti, and Madrigal, for your advice.
Erin Holman, for being such a great editor to work with.
My Favorites, the Authors and the People: You are the inspiration.
The United States of America, for the endless opportunities.
The University of Wisconsin Press, for The Opportunity.

As a nomad living in the most advanced nation on earth,
as a traveler skipping town without a savings account,
as a writer completing a book without a computer,
I've had to depend on many, many, many people.
I'm immensely grateful to each and every one of you
who gave me shelter, fed me,
and let me use your computers to type these pages from my note pads.

The names of people, institutions and places (except "Big") in the book
have been changed.

Translations

Amharic

Baleghe/Sid: Ill-mannered / ill-bred
Barya: Slave
Berbere: Hot pepper
Bir: Ethiopian currency
Dedeb/denkoro: Stupid/idiot
Dirya: A long loose dress (Somali outfit)
Emaye: Mom
Enat ghela: Mother body (Term of endearment)
Gabi: A large white scarf
Injera: Soft Ethiopian bread
Tchat: Green herb
Tej: Honey wine
Wet: Spicy Ethiopian dish

Arabic

Habibi: My dear
Wallahi: I swear
Al hamdu el Allah: Praise be to Allah
Bismillahi rahmani raheem: In the name of Allah, the all merciful and
　all compassion
Sami'a Allahu liman hamidah: Allah listens to him who praises him
As salamu alaikum wa rahmatu Allah: Peace and mercy of Allah be on
　you

French

Pommes: Apples
La fleur que tu m'avais jetée: The flower that you threw at me

Dans ma prison m'était restée: Stayed with me in my prison
Flétrie et sèche: Withered and dried
Cette fleur gardait toujours sa douce odeur: This flower kept its sweet
   fragrance.

Italian

Bar: Coffee shops in Italy
Canna: Joint
La metro: The subway
Maledetta: Damned
Merda: Shit
Negri: Blacks (a derogatory term)
Piazza: Square
Ragá: Short for *ragazzi,* guys
Ridere: To laugh
Soggiorno: Resident permit
Vaffanculo: Go fuck yourself.
Vino: Wine

Somali

Ma nabad baa: Is it peace? (a form of greeting)
Waa nabad: It is peace.

Spanish

Balsas: Rafts
Travieso: Mischievous
Traje de luz: Costume of the bullfighter (suit of light)

BLUE DAUGHTER OF THE RED SEA

Book 1

EXODUS OF BODIES

THERE IS A WET FEELING in between and on the back of my thighs and on my buttocks. I can tell clearly that it isn't pee since pee feels warm on the skin and this sensation is rather cool. I don't dare to ask the pharaoh for permission to use the restroom because he is in the middle of giving his students a lecture. I sure wouldn't want to endanger my behind to the exposure of his wooden stick. What if the wet material or liquid dripped down! The wet feeling intensifies on my skin, throughout my lower body. Tears swim in my eyes and I think how the punishment for crying for nothing, interrupting the flow of a lecture, would be at minimum a reproach accompanied by a few kisses thrown deliberately by a wooden ruler.

Meti, how many continents are there on earth?

The earth has stopped turning. I can hear the clock ticking, Tic-Toc-Tic-Toc-Tic, counting down the seconds that precede the end.

Meti, would you do us the courtesy of honoring us with your presence and tell us how many continents are there on earth?

Seven.

Can you name them?

I beg you thing under my feet swallow me would you please please please!

Boooom!!!!!!

Africa, Asia, Europe, North America, South America, Australia, and Antarctica.

I am invaded by the strangers that chose this moment and this room to conquer the territory around my thighs and my ass.

As with everything else, time comes to its end, and class is over. It's recess. The students run outside promptly as if the classroom is a cage and they are a flock of birds. I dodge my classmates and go to the restroom. Girls are lined up, each waiting for her turn to lock herself up in the tiny, private room, after those interminable hours in a crowded classroom.

They all seem to be engaged in a discussion about fashion: Oh, the things they'd do to their bodies once they got out of those damned uniforms. They would scrape their skin till any trace of baby-blue shirt and navy blue skirt disappeared. They would adorn their hair with beads and introduce their undeveloped breasts and virgin thighs to pink dresses.

I can't wait. I run to the administration office to ask for help to solve my confusion. But I can't bring myself to go past the door. I just stand by the wall and my hand stealthily reaches under my skirt and feels the back of my thigh. My fingers get a specimen of the wet stuff on my leg. It is yellow and flat, and it has invaded my thighs. For a moment, I consider the possibility it might be excrement, but I can't smell anything. And I can't possibly spoil the day for these people working in the office by asking them about the nature of the waste stuck to my skin. So I cry. Why do I have to bear such a slew of burdens? My peeing in bed. My high forehead, also known as Kilimanjaro by my brother's friends, and a subject of mockery for the young and the old. My inflated stomach, a trademark of the starving people. Let's not forget my imperfect form of speech, a stuttering tongue. And now, this flat, yellow stick falling like ice from the pores of my skin. Recess is over. The students run lazily back to their cages. I choose the promise of many a kiss from the wooden stick over the humiliation of walking in the classroom with yellow dew raining down my legs. I equip my heart with an armor and ask the woman at the front desk what is a flat, yellow thing that likes to stick to your thighs called? She can't quite understand my abstract question. Could I speak clearly? How can I speak clearly when, like Moses, I have been denied the leisure of fluent speech, and God hasn't bothered to provide me with a spokesperson named Aaron!

Young lady, speak up! Have you lost your tongue?

Have I lost my tongue? Of course, I have. I have lost it in the cruelty of your demeanor. It has been swallowed by the icy coldness of your glance, bashed into pieces by your fucking indifference, old lady. How do you expect me to speak up when your eyes have reduced me to a space that fills the nothingness that surrounds your office! How do you expect me to have a voice when you have stolen it from me and buried it in the backyard of your decaying thoughts of the day! How do you expect me to preserve a tongue when you and your kind have already determined my worth and have readied the location where you will categorize me! What use is an explanation for those like you who don't see beyond the surface of things! What use are words for those like me who exist in the forgotten realm of silence!

Instead, I use visual terms to make my question clear to the lady, and I show her the flat, yellow stick. The sight of the yellow character seems to offend her; yet, she forces an unnecessary smile and reveals the answer by means of a wry mouth. Those flat, yellow sticks are tapeworms. And the pores of my skin are not the source. It is my dirty stomach.

1

Light

(The Origins)

The Lord preceded them,
In the daytime by means of a column of cloud
to show them the way,
and at night by means of a column of fire
to give them light.

Exodus 13:21

THE CIRCUMCISED MARYS, THEY WERE CALLED, the young girls who
were exempted from going through circumcision. My mother was among
them. She spoke in a contented tone whenever she narrated that story to
me. For a devoted Catholic as mom was, there was nothing in the world
better than being labeled after the Virgin Mary, whichever way the name
might have been applied. And so my mother was a chosen Mary, I thought.

But why? I asked her. *What made you different? You and the other few.*

I don't know, she said. *They just examine your vaginal area carefully and
decide whether you need to be circumcised or not. If you are born already circumcised, then, you are a circumcised Mary and, therefore, you won't need to
be circumcised.*

Was I a circumcised Mary? I asked.

*I wouldn't know. When you were born, circumcision for girls was no longer
practiced. Only with boys.*

I imagined the faces of those girls who were doomed to subject their
vagina to the sharp-edged tooth of a knife. If Jesus was sacrificed for the
sins of the world, I thought, then, these women must have been sacrificed
for the same reason. We had Jesuses running around all over Ethiopia. My
mother was an exception. A circumcised Mary she was!

*So, tell me, mom! What was like to live at a time when such a thing as cir-
cumcision for women was practiced?*

*Well, first of all, we didn't have opportunities like you do. We didn't go to
school. Oh, yeah, my dear! You have an illiterate mother. Back then, we lived*

for today's bread. The future didn't lie ahead of us. We did not rely on ourselves. God was our everything. We didn't question our past. Our mothers didn't keep track of our age. We simply existed in the moment, within the limitations of our small town and small minds.

Poverty is venom that slowly saps one's existence. It is a white noise that quakes the shape of survival. It corrodes the scenery and cuts one's world asunder. I was born and grew up in the heart of that corrosive acid. Dire Dawa, a small city warmly embraced by a fiery sun and caressed by some magicless dust, was the name of my hometown. Life was not charming in Dire Dawa. Children ran barefoot against a background of feces-embedded roads, spinning around the desert city, puffing on the sand so forming dunes of smaller versions, while the little ones piggybacked on their mother's back. They had the appearance of several shiny, brown ponies: untamed and wild creatures. Their feet moved like those of a ballerina without her tutu, dancing to the tune of an unheeded song: free. Their laughter rang like a violent rain of diamonds. And they shouted in a language as inarticulate as their age, and yelled in voices as overly used as the sole of the shoe that was guarded at home for special occasions. The boys wandered nearly naked, their genitals covered with raglike shorts like savages from the jungle. The girls wore simple dresses, their undeveloped chests not yet choked by stifling brassieres. Their dust-devoured feet matched the soiled hands, their nasal mucus, the nappy hair that the sandy and adventurous day had transformed into strands of gray hair, and the clothes, previously immersed in mud. There were cuts all over their legs and ulcers noted on their knees, forming rings of pus. Lice walked on their head and tapeworms lived in their stomach.

When the boys were big enough for school, they had to subject themselves to circumcision. A noneducated but naturally gifted and self-trained expert did the surgery at home. The boys bawled and screamed as the prepuce was cut off. The best part came afterward, when they had to come out to play, wearing their sisters' dress, their testicles dangling like bells. We lifted the garments and laughed at the sight of the tiny genitals.

Our parents had our backs, evading despair by clinging to survival, making daisies out of faith. Religion was indeed an escape. The conviction of suffering in this world to be happy in the next one nurtured people's shattered hearts. Yet, reality lacked grace. Starvation stealthily ate away the veins of living. Ignorance paralyzed the mind. Idleness gnawed at the spirit.

Our neighborhood, Kezira, was nice. Or so it was considered by the denizens, tourists, and, of course, statistics. Nice was a lie. I used to walk up and down the asphalted, sticky streets and the muddy, filthy roads, and I would see more misery than nicety. My favorite stop was my grand-mother's, since most of my friends lived in the same condominium. What a condominium! Large families were massed into one-room apartments with walls that were an intersection between Cezanne's *Cracked House* and the Leaning Tower of Pisa. However, these lacked a painter's pigmentation or a landmark's everlasting attraction. Worse yet were the nonstop running noses of the kids and the frail skinny bodies and the dirty bare feet. I had then decided that I was better off than most of them because I lived in the big house. The House. I am not so sure whether I am entitled to call it my house. Nor do I know if my mother ever claimed that property as her own. Originally, it belonged to her late companion, an Italian warrior who wound up settling in the land he once coveted and attempted to vanquish but failed.

An endless, futile, dry underbridge that connects my neighborhood with the next one shoulders our house. It is dangerous to cross the road that lies under that bridge because a flood is expected at anytime. Many people who happen to walk across it at the wrong time are stolen away by those floods. But the worst homicides that those floods commit are the newborn babies who are often abandoned outside our house, down the hill, on the waterless underbridge. I suppose the mothers hope for the occasional flood to take them away to a better shore, somewhere in one of those foreign countries described in those fiction books my friend and classmate Shuni lends me to read. And there, perhaps, a beautiful, seminaked Egyptian queen will find him and beg her pharaoh-husband to make the kid in the basket a prince (even though these ones don't have the comfort of a bas-ket, but what does it matter as long as the baby gets in the hands of the gold-clothed queen?). Yet, this idea doesn't comfort me much when I hear the cry of those abandoned newborns, bawling themselves to death. In the mornings, I wake up to that awful sound of suffering, which forces me into a flow of quiet conversations with myself. Mental masturbation at an age when one can't even tell the difference between the abstract and the concrete can be as violent as rape. I shift my mind from one place to an-other, overwhelmed with certitudes of being listed in hell, where the devil is waiting to greet me, and all for the sin of my helplessness. I cry my days away. For no reason. Or that's what mom says whenever she sees me cry-ing. I will give you a reason to cry if you want, she shouts, as she gives me a taste of her violence-driven hands. I just walk away, resting my cool palm on my hot cheek. She wouldn't be able to understand my nameless pain. And I wouldn't be able to explain who fathers these thoughts and feelings of mine. But I am enlightened with a fruitful idea that requires me to communicate with mom. I ask her if we can adopt the forsaken children. She says that we can barely provide food for ourselves, let alone take care of thousands of abandoned babies.

I insist, *What about the orphanage; why can't the nuns take them?*

The nuns can only look after grown kids, says mom. She tells me to go mind my business. What did I know about raising babies! It requires too much work and time.

Meti, stop trying to save the world and go do your homework! It's an order!

I don't and can't understand anything about this world. I cannot comprehend how God could destroy places like the city of Sodom and Gomorrah for their wicked indulgence but let the city of Dire Dawa get away guiltfree when helpless babies are left out in the cold under bridges and inside the trash and denizens just cover their eyes and say that they barely have food for themselves and couldn't take care of motherless children and worse yet that the brides of God wouldn't do it because it requires too much work and time. If you ask me, God, this deserved a subtler punishment. But God is having a laugh from upstairs. To protest against His persistent indifference, I decide to go on a strike and ditch church to go over our neighbor Hajji to indulge myself with the sin of excess food. However, the generous act of one of our neighbors restores my faith. One crispy and sweet morning, Uzziel takes under her wing the forlorn child, and we kids are everyday at her one-room apartment, cooing and fondling the tiny fingers of the brand new child.

According to mom's gin-drinking clients' alcohol-driven tales, I was found under the bridge behind our house, in the middle of nowhere, where my natural mother abandoned me, and ever since mom has been taking care of me. They say that that explains the nature of my dark skin; and that compared to my sister and my brother, I look like a *barya*. They say that I have a good chance of passing for a *Falasha*, a black Jew, and I may as well try my luck in Israel because I'm certainly not of that house's blood.

You know, Meti, you'd be better off with your people. You'd fit in just right. Plus, they're filthy rich, these people. And you can find them wherever you go. They have found their kingdom in the Americas, Europe, and for all we know, they're probably the ones living at the base in Antarctica or giving tours in the

North Pole. But, little girl, you must always remember to say that your mother was the Jew. It doesn't make a difference if your father was one. You will understand these things when you grow up. For now just do as we say and go find your roots.

I know from experience that the account of my supposed ancestors' history is a brief introduction to the show of the evening.

Shall we play the game? asks one drunkard.

What was it called? I forgot, says another drunkard.

"*Where is Meti really from?*" shout the drunkards in unison.

There is an endlessly long pause filled with laughter.

No, no, no . . . I got a better one: "The origin of the child found under the bridge."

Too long. How about "The forgotten child"?

Ha Ha Ha Ha!!!! He He He He!!!!

Mom? My voice in its vain attempt to call for my mother's divine intervention.

Let them. They don't know what they're saying, says the lady, imitating Christ, before she walks to the kitchen to replace the empty bottle of gin with a full one.

What is it they're saying without knowing? asks the newcomer who is stepping into mom's verandah and makes himself comfortable on the floor as he shouts his order of a glass of gin.

We are writing the history of the forgotten child.

You mean the adopted one in the house?

Shhh . . . It's a secret!

Sometimes I cry when hearing their version of my life story. Sometimes I laugh. After all, they're all jokers. They would transform that verandah into a comedy stand and themselves into Emmy-winning comediennes. We have no TV; thus, they are true entertainers for me. However, often, their shows are at my expense. They give an account of my unusual birth circumstances in so many forms and so repetitively, I have a hard time not believing it. But, on the weekend, if I've been irresistibly good during the week, Mom gives me permission to go watch TV over our neighbor Hajji's house, and that way I take a break from hearing the story of my early life recounted by those drunkards. Instead, I watch Bruce Willis and Cybill Shepherd attack each other in *Moonlighting*. It is like laughing at silent movies because I can't understand a word they say. They speak in English.

On Saturday nights, the channel airs a comedy show in Amharic. The show is a simpler, Ethiopian version of *Saturday Night Live*. The performers don't seem to wear make up. The lighting is bleak, and the sound is poor. I fall in love with that small box that miraculously spits images of living people and caricatures. And I place my life in the ongoing adventures of those caricatures; that way I cease to be a bastard and assume the role of a cartoon animated picture.

As I sit on the verandah, cross-legged, facing the group of drunken men, a train of thoughts starts its journey in my head. Why do I have to deal with these people? I know for a fact that drinking alcohol is a sin. Then, why is mom, a devoted Catholic, selling alcohol at night on our verandah? I don't dare to ask her such a question. It would be same as claiming her to be a sinner, and I know what that would bring. So instead, I study her movements painstakingly. I notice how she ever wears a solemn look on her rather dark face. I watch how, as she pours gin in her clients' cups, she knits her eyebrows slightly, as if offended by the same alcohol smell she has been experiencing for years. I turn my inspecting eyes to the boys who are laughing and shouting words raised by a shameless and brave single parent named gin. I have to be careful when looking at them so intently or worse yet when laughing at their jokes. I might attract their attention and before I know it the joke will be on me. And that is exactly what happens. One of them has already started to tell his version of my birth tale. He claims and swears that mom first spotted me while I was sitting beside a beggar. Mom felt so much pity for me and my big eyes evoked such tenderness in her that she couldn't just walk away once she put the coins in my supposed natural mother's cup for alms. She stopped and made a deal with the beggar, and here I am, the fruit of that bargain. He says that most probably I'm wondering why I'm so dark and my sister and brother so fair. Well, I don't have to wonder anymore about that. Thanks to his good memory and kind gesture of retelling a forsaken story, I can finally rest my whys in peace. I have an answer now: I am a bastard. I am a beggar. I don't even belong in this house. Many a thought crosses my mind as I listen to his cruel words. I think how I want to tear this fucking jerk to pieces and make him suffer the same pain that he is making me feel at that moment. I make love to the ideas of spitting at him, slapping him, and strangling him until he experiences every reaction that he is causing inside me. But my thoughts remain where they are conceived, and the only reaction I succeed to evoke in that drunkard is a wicked laugh.

The stories told by mom's drunken clients are not based on pure imagination. In Dire Dawa, it is common for homeless people to steal kids to use them as piteous images that'd evoke the passersby to pour a coin or two in their cup for alms. My friend and neighbor Reuben's little brother gets lost and is nowhere to be found. Each of us runs to various parts of the city, looking for him. We kids look for him in all the hiding places that we use whenever we play hide and seek; but he's not there. He's not running about the market coveting for food, either. He's not in any of the restaurants and cafes we kids sneak into, then be kicked out in our attempt to experience rich people's treat of dining out. He's nowhere near or far in the places anyone can think of. However, as the day comes to its end and our search reaches a point of despair, we find him on the sidewalk of a bridge, sitting beside a homeless woman, a beggar, who claims him to be her son and would these strangers please stop yanking her child away from her. It's her child. She bore him in her womb for nine months. For heaven's sake, she can't even sit in peace, begging for money so that she can feed her starving baby. The women from my neighborhood shout at her words of insults and reproach. The just-found child's mother grabs the beggar's hair and readies her hand to hit her, but someone holds her back. The beggar runs down the bridge. Everyone else stays with the little boy for a while: some kissing him, others stating heatedly their opinions on what they all just experienced. I, for my part, am lost in the labyrinth of my story. So where did all begin? Whose daughter was I to begin with? From whom did the homeless woman steal me before she used me as a piteous image for her begging, which was when my present mother saw me for the first time and fell in love and bought me?

But, in reality, I am not the fruit of a bargain between my mother and a homeless woman. I am the fruit of a political treaty. My mother remembered the day I was conceived to be a glorious one. My father was a colonel, a man with many powers, among which was to save mom's nephew. A man who was given political power to persecute people introduces my father-to-be to my mother before questioning her about a certain political party formed by young people who opposed the government of the time. Mom was suspected of hiding important information and evidence from the authority. The persecutor was famous for taking young workers from big companies to search, arrest, and kill them. The persecutor and the colonel phoned mom and came to see her at the house once and again, demanding to know whether she knew anything about the underground parties. Mom answered no to their incessant questions. But, in the process, she fell fully in love with the colonel and he with her. But there was an obstacle that impeded their love: he was taken. Nevertheless, the day arrived when heaven sent down a reason for them to be together and make me. Two of mom's nephews got arrested. Mom ran to her forbidden love and implored him to save her nephews' lives. The one who was to become my father imposed a condition to execute mother's solicitous request: she had to have sex with him. He said he knew it was a heavy thing to ask and gave her time to think about it. Days after that intense encounter, mom's nephew sent her a note hidden inside a plate with leftovers. The note read: *Auntie, the young men who are here with me are being killed one by one and I am waiting for my turn. Please, beg the colonel to talk with the persecutor since they're very good friends.*

Mom called the object of her affection and told him she accepted his indecent proposal. And out of that lovemaking, I was made. Hence, that day of body entwining and soul bewitching saved the life of an existing one and was the giver of a new life.

2

Appetizer

Any small portion that stimulates a desire for more
or that indicates more is to follow.

Webster's Unabridged Dictionary

WE THANKED THEM SIMULTANEOUSLY, in a choir. After all, it was a whole meal. We sat on the floor, our little bodies, which housed our eager hands and hungry stomachs, surrounding the big plate of food. Our small fingers grabbed as much rice and beef as they could and transported the morsels to our mouths. We looked like a group of contestants on a mission to see who would finish the food first. In reality, it was our stomachs that competed for that food. And the only prize they strove for was the award of being fed. The Somali rice with beef tasted delicious. We licked our fingers ingratiatingly, showing as much love to the relics of food as its flavor permitted. We vacillated in our state of belligerence and clemency. We resented our hosts. They never had to compete for leftovers. They never had to search for flavor in the dirty nails of their greasy fingers. They never had to beg. We watched them with envy and endeavored to forgive them their fault of needlessness. We appeased our warring thoughts with a dose of fantasy. We fabricated castles and crowned ourselves princes and princesses. Perhaps, life had hope in store for us. Perhaps, someday we too will be hosts to starving kids.

I was at Hajji's house. He was the blind aristocrat who owned both the house and the granary that stood in front of my house. So, while his family sold the grain that made Hajji wealthy and fed the poor and thus adorned his name with a valuable gem named good reputation, mom sat across from his house, selling potatoes sandwiches and gin to the hungry and tired working-class men. Hajji's house became the scenario for my fantasies. Everything he owned, I owned; every excursion his family took, I took; every whim they indulged, I indulged myself. I made up my mind to be the architect of my own world. And if window-shopping was the only alternative to enjoy life, then I had to shape my mind into a transparent glass through which to see my own version of the world.

Smell is my hometown's legacy to me. Smell of Somali rice, the memory of which clings to my fingers that I know and then lick, remembering the taste. Smell of dashed potatoes and hot-spiced *berbere* and fresh bread. Smell of onion chopped in tiny pieces and cooked with oil and melted butter until it is dark and ready to pour the hot *berbere* into and again to wait a while to mix the chicken or the lentils and other spices that make up the traditional Ethiopian dish *wet*. Smell of flour, which in a matter of minutes converts into a round, spongy, many-eyed *injera*. Smell of men's sweat, of people who flow to our house and ebb back to work, after appeasing the growling cries of their stomachs. Smell of excrement that often besieges the wall that separates our house from the futile field. Smell of hashish, which the men at Hajji's smoke inside the one room where they gather to converse and relax. Smell of *tchat* that my brother and his friends chew on late in the afternoon, sitting on the floor, by the gate of our house, and experience the emptiness of oblivion that only *tchat* can transmit. Smell of gin and *tej,* which invade our verandah through the foul breath of mom's drunken clients, as they cheer and narrate many a tale in a state of pure abandonment. Smell of blood, which automatically plants roots of knots in my throat and branches of weakness throughout my legs. Smell of my own self, so strong for lack of hygiene, shower being taken once a week. Smell of my mother, a mixture of sweat and food aromas, scent that harrows me wherever I go.

The shit is at arm's reach wherever I go. As I squat down on the floor, I feel the air caress my nakedness and the dirt make its way up into my ass, and I immerse myself in the foul smell. I have to make room for the next person and make sure that I am not invading the space of those who were there before me. We form a queue: a group of squatting animals, gorillas perhaps, or monkeys. It is liberating. The release of waste. The intercourse with the open air. The blue-eyed sky watching us. The earth touching us. The flies invading the territory around us. I breathe it all in, the nature and the misery in its purest essence: the shit, the flies, the sky, and the sleazy dirt. The final act requires more creativity. It is a matter of taste. Sometimes, we indulge ourselves with newspapers, the soft feeling deep in the crack of our asses. Other times, we use a piece of rock to cleanse the yellow character, an experience of rape. The shit smears like cream on the stone. And there are also those times when we walk away with an ass as virgin as an unshaved face.

There is food in my kitchen, but its mere smell, which suggests a world of repetition, drives me across the street to Hajji's. Mom is not happy that I eat at Hajji's. The meat they eat, which most of their dishes consist of, is not blessed. Mom reminds me repetitively that, while the cows and goats and sheep whose meat we Christians eat are killed by an assassin who makes the sign of the cross and asks our Father to bless it, the Muslims consult their Allah. And for all she knows, Allah isn't my God.

You have a God of your own, don't you forget that.
Mom, what's the difference between God and Allah?
God is your god and Allah is not.

Oh, if mom only knew how I praise their Allah, sneaking in their mosques, thanking Him for granting me the Hajjis for neighbors. *Al Hamdu El Allah.*

Bismillahi rahmani raheem.
Sami'a Allahu liman hamidah.
Al salamu alai kum wa rahmatu Allah.

If she only knew how intently I study their ritual, how I try to memorize the unintelligible phrases that come out of my neighbors' mouths, to practice them later in case my conversion brings the miracle of a second birth with the silver spoon in my mouth.

Why does he wash himself so much before prayer? I ask Fatima, Hajji's wife, as I follow her in and out of the room while she readies the chamber pot for her husband. Hajji's son is outside with a bucket filled with water. He washes his face. His mouth and nostrils. His hands and arms and elbows. His feet and ankles. He rubs his head with water. He heads to the living room, rolls out a prayer rug, raises his hands up to the level of his ears, bows down with hands on knees, sits up, and then falls prostrate, with his head to the ground.

Because water purifies the body like the prayer purifies the soul.
On top of being blind, Hajji must be something else, because he is confined to his bed at all times. On our way to Hajji's room, I ask Fatima whether Hajji is bedridden because of his eyes or because of the something else and if so does this something else have a name and a definition.

He is paralyzed. He can't move on his own. He needs me and his wheelchair.
My second favorite part of Hajji's room is the carpet. So rich of colors and designs and so full of birds and flowers and trees. A Persian rug. My first

favorite thing is the smell. So rich of aromas and spices and perfumes and foods.

Hajji mumbles something in Somali when he senses my presence in the room.

Aklile's daughter, replies Fatima.

Ma nabad baa?

Waa nabad.

I help Fatima get Hajji out of the bed and to the chamber pot that is waiting clean and ready on the floor beside the bed.

Fati?

Yes, Meti.

Why is it that lots of Muslim men are called Hajji?

Because they have made the pilgrimage.

What's the pilgrimage?

A journey to Mecca.

Where is Mecca?

In Saudi Arabia. Right next to the Red Sea.

Why is it a big deal to visit Mecca?

Because it's the birthplace of Muhammad. He is the founder of Islam.

My conspiracy only gets me in trouble. I am back to church. The priest reminds his audience that the True Faith is indeed Catholicism. The Lord be praised! The images of hell that were engraved in me at Catechism, the fire that I would end up in for eternity if I didn't get my priorities straight run before my eyes. Being a Catholic comes first. The least I can do is limit my immersion in the Islamic world to my excursions to gather food. But mom warns me that I'd better eat whatever it's in the house. Beggars can't be choosers. And there goes again in my head the question on my origin. But I choose not to entertain myself too much with thoughts of beggars and illegitimate births. Better to ignore mom and think of ways to get to Hajji's house. What does mom know about a child's desires! How the smell of spicy beef and rice from across the street entices my stomach! How for months I pray for Ramadan to approach our town so that I can have the best food ever at Hajji's! How I would gladly be adopted by a rich mulatto family so that I can eat as many *pommes* as I crave for without receiving any demeaning looks by those foreign women who sell imported goods! How I wish for a different life, a second birth, a pair of rich parents, and a bunch of cabinets filled with food and food and only food!

Glycerin is a clear oily lotion to moisturize the hands, legs, and body. Or at least that's what mom uses it for. She is extremely economical with it and uses small portions when her skin gets extremely dry. The lotion tastes so sweet that I can't stop myself from drinking a few sips every day. Mom doesn't know that I drink it, but she is not happy that her lotion is being wasted so recklessly by me when my skin doesn't even need any moisture.

Meti, how many times do I have to tell you to quit indulging your skin with my glycerin?

OK, mom!

OK, what?

OK, I will no longer indulge my skin with your glycerin.

Mom gives me a look that I am very familiar with and I have long ago decided to name it "the assassin look." But my stomach couldn't care less about the assassin look each time it gets close to the glycerin. It grows legs and runs for the liquid to experience the orgasm that's reached when the yearning for sweet meets the moment of moisture.

Aaai have a se-cret! I sing/confess to my playmates.

Meti, your secrets are always boring and stupid, one of them replies.

Denkoro! Anyhow, my very interesting and quite phenomenal secret is that you no longer have to steal to get a taste of sweet flavors. You can find it right in your house.

Boring! Stupid! repeats the idiot.

Tell us your secret, another one says patronizingly.

Glycerin. I have been drinking my mother's lotion, and it's delicious. You got to absolutely try it.

Eew! I can't believe you've been drinking lotion. That's disgusting!

You eat mud all the time, dedeb!

But that's different. Mud is cool. That's where food grows.

I still think you're an idiot.

And I still think your secrets are boring and stupid.

In spite of my friends' disgust with my drinking of the lotion and mom's warnings and assassin looks, I can't stay away from the glycerin. I am so addicted to the pleasure that I gain from drinking it that I can't get enough of it. And since the piggy bank that mom keeps in the room is not always generous to my malign, stealing hands, glycerin is the only sweet taste that my tongue can afford to experience for days or weeks. And I take it drop by drop, smearing my tongue with the fluid, mixing it with my saliva and swallowing it down my throat as if it were my last indulgence before death.

While glycerin serves to curb my craving for sweets, mud gives my

friends and me access to a world of meals. We cook make-believe beef-
steaks, and meatballs, perfecting the shape of each small round ball with
water. We serve ourselves a few servings, using sticks from trees as forks
and knives. We eat pieces of mud and think our action exciting, for we feel
pretty independent and quite some cooks.

Ummm . . . It's delicious!

Can I have more?

I only got one meatball. He's got three.

Can we do this more often? It's more fun than eating at home.

In some cases, life's limitations can make the prerequisites for happiness
easily attainable.

Mom saves change in the piggy bank that she keeps in the bedroom. It isn't
an easy task to get the coins out, yet, a day doesn't pass by without me sneaking in the bedroom and shaking the cup until it spits enough change for
me to buy ice cream or something like it. I hide the sin when I go to confession, for all the priests in that church know me and I wouldn't be able
to look them in the eyes ever again if I confessed about my stealing. So I
prepare a script that presents me in a better light than the truth would.

*Father, forgive me, for I have sinned! I had a fight with my friends. I disre-
spected my mother. I forgot to pray. I was not 100 percent focused during mass.*

There goes my chance of being purged! I just wasted an opportunity to
reconcile with God. I can feel myself sinking in the sleazy dirt of unspo-
ken truths, swimming in a sea of guilt. And I hate my hometown for con-
fining us to just one Catholic church, where everyone knows everyone,
thus denying us the freedom to escape to foreign confessional boxes to
pour our dirty deeds to a stranger with a crown and a gift to absolve.

When class is over for the day, students run outside the gate to buy ice
cream and cookies or candies to proudly eat on the way home. If the piggy
bank hasn't been generous enough to let me steal a bunch of coins, I have
to watch, empty-handed, the excruciating scene of these gluttons munch-
ing delicious cookies. I walk home, holding my tears back, praying with
an intensity only children can master when they pray for their wishes to
come true that some day soon I'd be rich enough to show off like the rest
of my classmates. When I get home, I take off my horrible uniform and
change into ordinary clothes. I run outside and cross the dry underbridge
to join the group of children who, since they are not able to afford to go
to school, made the shade under a tree their learning center. Two of the
kids who frequent the school under the tree sleep on our veranda at night.

They tell me to quit raising my hand to answer the questions that the generous, unpaid, self-taught, untitled teacher asks.

You don't even belong here. You're one of them. You have already been given the answers. We are here to learn. Not to boast.

But I participate anyway, showing off, feeding my ego with the fat that is extracted from the self-obsessed product that I have turned into.

When the one-hour class is over, we get up from the muddy floor (their seats), and if necessary, run to the corner to wee-wee or excrete and use rocks in lieu of toilet paper. We spread into different directions to go home, and my momentary happiness is gone like a drug that wears away. The idea of relating to these kids more than to the kids I go to school with scares me somehow. I am interested in banishing the curse of poverty, not in being involved. But the status of my clothes, the lice in my hair, my inflated stomach, the absence of a TV and a decent couch in the house, the neglect of a monthly allowance, are all characteristics of the poor. And heaven forbid that I be one.

Everyone has a pen friend who lives in a first-world country. I can't afford to have one because it requires envelopes, stamps, and shipping expenses since the two corresponding parties exchange cultural souvenirs and courteous gifts. I am so jealous of my classmates I am at risk of exploding. And when I get home, my presence is completely ignored. Mom is busy grieving over either the prior night's tragedy or anticipating the following night.

Mom, I no longer own a heart.

Ahah . . .

Mom, I am converting into a beast.

Ahah . . .

Mom, I am getting a divorce from life.

Ahah . . .

I take comfort in my books, but the fact that the characters live such intriguing lives with happy ending irritates me. What irritates me even more is the detailed description of the French interior decoration or the numerous pieces of silverware and glasses set on the table for a single person. Do we readers need to know if the characters in the book use one glass for wine and another for water? For God's sake, enough with leisurely living! I cry day in and day out. Then, I am filled with an excellent idea that requires making stealing a habit. But this time, I'd use the money for a more meaningful purpose than buying ice cream after school. I go to buy school supplies and take them home to show them to mom. I invent a name of a foreign white girl in my head and choose the country she is from (Germany), and I tell mom how she sent me the school supplies. Mom and everyone else are proud of me that I got myself a pen friend from a first-world country. Again, my pride and joy are so momentary they don't last the effect of a drug. I suffer within, bearing three crosses: the awareness that I have no real pen friend, the harrowing feeling of guilt, and the painful state of imagining what kind of punishment the coupling of stealing and lying would bring upon me.

I attend funerals to forget about my life. The frequent marches to the cemetery are long but exciting. The coffin is carried from our church to the house of tombs. I enjoy this ritual of accompanying the dead to his resting haven. The cemetery is my favorite place in Dire. It feels like home among the dead. I adore the silence. I adore the goosebumps that the presence of the dead people evokes on my skin. I adore the dead people, their foreign past and faces. "From dust to dust" rings in my head as if to remind myself of my own insignificance. My joy in tasting the delicious fragrance of glycerin on my tongue, in reading books that describe foreign cultures, in feeding my cravings with wishful thinking, are all useless and a waste of time. I should focus, instead, on the Bible and its teachings. I shall memorize a psalm a day. I shall consult Genesis on the origin of man; scrutinize Exodus till I am guided to the Promised Land. I shall make of the church my principal home. I shall attend all masses and pay my most undivided attention to the sermons. I shall punish myself severely whenever my mind goes a-wandering in regions of mundane elements. I shall no longer say profanities or lie or steal or miss mass or eat at Hajji's. All these promises I make as I follow the crowd of people who lead the funeral procession. The trip to the cemetery is like a trip to the inside of a grave. It is a process of sinking into a ditch. I am going to meet the dead, converse with them, pour out a little of my sadness and a little of my happiness. The grave is the point of nowhere. All those buried bodies are not really there. I try to place them somewhere in my head, find a niche for them to rest in without having to wander restlessly in inhospitable spaces or having to wait for the pitch darkness to fall upon the sky in order to visit their loved ones. I feel not a grip of pain or pity for the one lying inside the coffin. I only wonder on the whereabouts of his soul. Is he on his way to heaven or hell? Has she been good or bad? But he and she don't keep the chords of my interest awake for long. I am more in awe of the ones already lying under the ground. The ones that have experienced the other world for the past days, months, years. What does this one knows about being dead? He hasn't even left the premises of the ground. So I imagine the tombs to be cages filled with people, and they open wide the city of imagination in my head. I create heaven, a large bed of white flowers and peopled with white-gown-clothed angels. And hell, a pit parted in two parts, sulfur raging with fire and an iceberg. I ponder the two images of unbearable heat and gelid cold, ambivalent which to choose in case I venture into hell in the future. I run to the tombs, sit on them, knock with the hope that someone might answer from inside, show me in. A shudder lingers in my body. A person who once existed, lived in this fucked-up city, had a body and a mind, is lying beneath the soil. Someday, I too will join him. And once again, I shiver from the idea of turning into soil, the fear of no longer being part of the world someday, the certainty of being nothing.

3

Reformatory Sessions

One is not born a warrior,
You become one.

Arab proverb

MAKING WHAT WAS BENT STRAIGHT was the motto of our schools and families. Neither our teachers nor our parents tolerated flaws. We were born impeccable, and we had to remain thus. We were given no allowances to be careless, to make mistakes, to stumble over a stone. We were not permitted to ask questions, to inquire, to have a thirst for knowledge. The possibilities of other worlds were closed to our access. We could exist only within the limitations of the space we were able to see in the not-by-choice experience of lowering our heads, from which position we counted empires of ants. At home, there were the Ten Commandments to follow, and many more made up by the earthly parents.

> Thou shall not live!
> Thou shall not breathe!
> Thou shall not speak!
> Thou shall not have a mind!
> Thou shall not eat in excess!
> Thou shall not jump overboard!
> Thou shall not walk over the border!

Failure to carry them out meant hours of physical torture. At school, the smallest deed was a felony that needed to be punished. It could be forgetting to do our homework, failing to answer a question, speaking when we were not asked to, or doing anything that the teacher thought was inappropriate. Different teachers had diverse standards for crime and punishment. Some made the errant student go in front of the class and take off his pants or lift her skirt to make sure no extra garment was hidden beneath for protection and then hit the student's buttocks with a big piece of wood.

Another type of punishment was to spend the entire period in a corner or in front of the class, where you had to squat down, put your hands across the back of your legs and between your inner thighs, and reach up to your ears. You were to stay for the full hour in that position, your hands holding your ears, your face facing the class, your buttocks pointing at the blackboard and your legs slightly bend, trembling like a leaf in the wind. It was in those classrooms that the root of forbearance was planted in me.

The teacher holds the ruler, mom the switch, dad-non-dad the belt. And I count the one hundred steps to death. I have got a magical pill in my head. I am planning to use it to stop the pain that will come from 1. The Ruler. 2. The Switch. 3. The Belt. There is fear gripping the cords in my throat. I am choking, choking to death. I say a prayer, but God won't come to my rescue. I close my eyes, but I can still picture the shape of the wooden stick, the swing of the switch, and the flight of the belt. The tears come undulating on my cheeks, releasing one thousand years of solitude. I gain strength from morals carried in the aftermath of things. I am at home on my way to school, and I am anticipating the wrongdoings of the day. I am counting the one hundred steps to death, one by one, all the way to school. The pharaoh has a power on me no one will ever know. He rules all the keys to my emotions. One word from him and I will reach out for the ropes and fasten them tight. I've to secure the middle ground of my sanity. One—two—three. . . . My thoughts. How can I hinder my head from brooding thoughts of death under the hurling lashes of a wooden ruler? Seven—eight—nine. . . . Reminder: Remember to take the magic pill. Thirteen—fourteen—fifteen. . . . Mom is in one of her notorious melancholic moods. She won't talk to me. She won't look at me. She is in a voyage of prayers. Days like this, I am scared of her, of her oblivious state and death-like presence. Thirty-seven—thirty-eight—thirty-nine, . . . I'm shaking. I don't want to leave the house. I don't want to face the pharaohs and those braying kids, my classmates. But mom's mere presence is sufficient to drive me away. Anywhere but here. Anywhere but home. Home has become a place of solitude. The maternal bosom is no longer a refuge. No asylum is granted in mom's land of agonies. Fifty-nine—sixty—sixty-one. . . The street is one big motion picture of misery. Children so skinny and so dirty it hurts the eyes. Stomachs bulging, eyes piercing with the intensity of sadness, hands swinging like reeds, noses shedding soluble liquid, lips flaking crumbs of skin. I refuse to be part of this crowd. I refuse to expose my bulging stomach in public. I refuse to let my nose run wild and mingle with the flakes from my lips. I refuse! I refuse! I refuse! I shut my eyes tight and make a wish. I wish for a flat stomach, a dry nose, and a pair of moist lips. I wish for the advantage-ridden universe of exceptional things. Eighty-six—eighty-seven—eighty-eight. . . . The more privileged of my classmates are fabricating new jokes, brand-new names for my high forehead and inflated stomach over my skinny body. Ninety-two—ninety-three—ninety-four. . . . The lesson begins. The pharaoh presents his lectures first, and then his questions. Everyone tries his best to live up to his expectations. We shape and polish our responses, make them so irresistible he can't reject them. Our effort is vain. Someone comes along and ruins it all. *He can't remember. She forgot. Oh, I thought that was the definition of an atom.* And we all must pay the consequences for those people's mistakes. Ninety-five—ninety-six—ninety-seven. . . . Line up. About face! Ninety-eight—ninety-nine. . . . The magical pill. Think of the magic pill, Meti. You won't feel a thing. The magic pill will protect you from any pain. Isn't that why it was invented? One hundred. . . . Boom! Boom! Boom! Magic pill fails. Everything fails.

The teacher we fear the most is our science instructor. He has no pity on us. He shouts at us to stand up and place our hands on the desk. Next, he orders us to bend our finger so that the tip of our fingers and the palm of our hands lie against the table, leaving the knuckles slightly aloof. Then, he draws closer to each one of us and cunningly brushes the knuckles with his long wooden ruler, lifts the weapon up in the air, seizes the landing, and hits successfully the same spot he set for, constraining the bend to unbend. He repeats the premeditated punishment once and again, and the more one cries and complains, the worse it gets; thus the battle is with intolerance, saying to yourself and often begging yourself to swallow the tears and stifle the sobbing.

Mom, I want to be fat.
And why is that?
Because the mean boys are afraid of fat girls.
Sahr is skinny and aren't the boys afraid of her?
That's cuz she's a fat girl's sister.
Meti!
I am serious. Can you make me fat? Please!
But you're always complaining about your belly.
My belly only makes me look like a freak. I want to be fat all over. I want to look intimidating.

OK, then. Eat lots of meat.

I do as mom says. I clean the plate that she serves me. I visit Hajji's more often. I pray: *Dear God, I beg you, make me fat.* But no results. No answer from God. No protruding thighs and arms from the meat that I eat. Still a reed with a bump in the middle. And the song goes on.

Her belly is so big.
Oh, so out of proportion.
Her arms so skinny.
Oh so so skinny.
Her lips so dry.
Oh so so dry.
Her nose is so large.
Oh so so large.
Her eyes so weird.
Oh so so weird.
She is so ugly.
Oh so so ugly.

I ask mom if I can please join the school of the poor.

There's no such thing.

What about the shade under the tree by Shuni's house?

That is not a school. And what is my problem? Can't I spend a day without creating a problem out of pure air?

I don't want to go to school with rich people anymore.

You're not going to school with rich people.

Then, how come they don't have big bellies, skinny arms, and dry lips? How come I am the only muse for their songs in the entire school? How come they have more than one uniform?

Meti, you know what you're doing, don't you?

Yes. Insulting God with my ingratitude. Because, after all, he granted me the fortune of health, never let me go to sleep hungry or abandoned me without a roof over my head and blah, blah, blah.

Her assassin look follows my blah, blah, blah. But I can't care less about the consequences of my very legitimate accusation. What did I do to deserve this? What did I do to be humiliated like that by those braying donkeys? And I come home hoping for some support, but I have to hear my mother preach about God. Did I ask anything about God? Can't God stay out of it for once? You're insulted and you're ungrateful if you don't let the insults sing you to silence. You complain and you're insulting God. You eat with people who are not affiliated with Christianity and you're offending

God. I am weary of fearing God. I am weary of being blamed for someone else's lack of sportsmanship.

Mom and the vampire take turns teaching me a lesson from my mistakes, as well as my teachers. Mom's fury is unprecedented and travels at full speed. I make the mistake of going a-wandering in the city with my friends. When I come back, mom greets me with the face of a fiend. She tosses the belt heedlessly all over me. And when even that doesn't appease her anger, she grabs my hair and throws me on the floor. She ties me up against a slender wood that stands like a pole in our verandah. She wraps the rope around my shoulder and around my lower body all the way down to my feet. She cuts a switch from one of our trees and comes back for me.

> *Laaaash . . . For daring to disobey me!*
> *Laaaash . . . For being irresponsible!*
> *Laaaash . . . For going a-wandering like a vagabond!*
> *Laaaash . . . For making me worried!*
> *Laaaash . . . For all the horrible images your absence caused to play in my head!*
> *And laaaash and laaaash and laaaash and laaaash and laaaash to infinity.*

She hits me until every skin on my body shivers with pain and my howling becomes an echo and my eyes are numb from weary tear glands. She leaves me hanging there for the rest of the evening. I am not allowed to say a word. I am not to be given any food. When everyone is gone, including her gin-drinking clients, and she is ready to sleep, she unties me and lets me go to sleep on the bed so that the night-wandering fatal insects wouldn't take out of me the life that she barely spared me.

The vampire's bedroom is as dark as night at all times. That man-non-man seems to be afraid of the light, and I wonder where he gets the courage to face the day. I always spend an awful lot of time with him in the room, and mom lets me. But this time, she must have heard something I failed to understand because she's outside, on the veranda, shouting my name, ordering me to come out. When I step into the veranda, I run into a number of people sitting on the floor, sipping on their coffee. Mom is waiting for me, holding a belt.

What were you conspiring about in there?
Nothing, mom.

Don't you play the fool with me and tell me what were you two talking about?

Everything, mom. School and. . . .

Since when did you become the spy of the house?

I am not a spy. I don't know what you're talking about. I don't know what you want from me.

I want you to keep your mouth shut; and I want you to stay away from that man. Is that too much to ask, eh?

She beats me heedlessly, screaming that I am forbidden to talk politics with that man. I cry, and when I see the cuts on my arms, I swear in God's name that I don't know what she is talking about. But she hits me harder, yelling at me not to ever dare call the name of God in vain. She makes me promise that I will never again listen a word about politics coming from that man. Even though I know nothing about politics except maybe the fact that the subject is somehow related to the police, jail, rifles, and the frequent visits we are paid late at night at home, I promise mom that I will never again engage in conversations about politics with the vampire. Bearing my fresh wounds on my skin, I resolve to go to the living room/bedroom, lie on the bed, and cry, wondering what exactly in my conversation with the vampire had turned out to be about politics. And I hate life for reducing me to an everlasting wondering, without ever understanding the meaning of what goes around me.

Now, it's the vampire's turn to beat me. We're in his room talking, and once again I must have said something despicable or grotesque because he flies to the door where his pants are hanging, takes his belt, and comes for me. He is hitting me with the belt. I don't fear him as much I fear mom, so I yell at him to stop. Mom hears me yelling and shouts my name from outside. But he's hitting me so hard I am on the floor, with my hands wrapped around my face, sobbing, my voice gone from too much crying. He stoops to take my hands off my face, and, pointing his index finger at me, he tells me to never again, he repeats, never dare I say that again. I sob harder, letting bizarre sounds out of my unopened mouth. But this time I am crying not out of physical pain but out of desperation. I am tired of being hit for reasons unknown to me. How am I supposed to never again say something if I don't even know what is it? Mom beats me for talking about something she calls politics when I can't even remember hearing it mentioned. Dad-non-dad nearly takes the life out of me for having said bad things, while I have no idea what they are. I just sit on the floor, moaning, rocking my body, and making an excruciating effort not to enter the pit of wondering. He leaves the room and evidently the house because mom comes to his room to get me. She takes me out on the veranda and her coffee-time friends look at me, uttering sounds of disbelief at whatever they're seeing on my momentarily disfigured face and arms. And I despise them for being so damn nosy, and I hate mom for letting this happen, and I am disgusted with myself for being so stupid as to let inappropriate things out of my mouth.

Be wary of the things that come out of your mouth. Be wary of the things that come out of your mouth. Be wary of the things that come out of your mouth. Conversations with myself are becoming more and more frequent. I must engrave in my green head that silence is a golden rule. *Silence is a golden rule. Silence is a golden rule. Silence is a golden rule.* It's actually not so difficult to understand the psychology behind rules at this age. If there were no rules, there would be no games. No hide and seek. No hopscotch. No rope jumping. No volleyball. That's it. A perfect metaphor for life: a game. From now on, I shall live as if I were playing a game. You want silence from me, then, silence be it. But be careful, for I will internalize every movement of yours and photograph every flight of your unprecedented fury. Be careful, for I will spell you out on the blank pages of my mind. I shall know you inside out. I will have no pity for you. You will mean nothing to me. You want silence from me, silence you'll have. And if you see me not moved by your tears not broken in the face of your sorrow not shriveled by the loss of you, remember that I am being loyal to your wish and to my promise to keep silence.

I am beginning to think that every lash from mom's switches, every slap from her hand, every smack from my teachers' wooden ruler is causing me to imagine things. I am imagining people to be devils. And if they're devils, then it's no sin to hate them. I shall hail the pages of hatred.

> One for my mother: for all the slaps, the lashes, and the assassin looks.
> One for my teachers: for all the beatings and the gift of eternal fear.
> One for the priests: for all the wrong information and the wrong accusations.
> One for the nuns: for all the threats and the thoughtless words.

But I discover that hatred isn't so powerful. There's no gain. Just a waste of energy. I hate and hate and hate and I am left with nothing but more hate and anger and with no strength to do anything else. Everyone is so in-volved in his own world he doesn't even notice you are piling hate at his feet. Fuck hatred! Coast down on the magic pill instead. The magic pill turns the world. You are transformed by the magic pill. Once it is in your system, the planet is at your feet. No more humiliations. No more bend-ing to offer your ass to the fury of a stick. No more terms of endearment to buy acceptance. No more seducing moms, teachers, friends, gods, priests, nuns, brothers, sisters, cousins . . . I shall make no effort. I shall be elusive. I shall live without the least consideration to make room for reality.

4

God and Satan

We work on the surface,
the depths are a mystery.

Bahaya proverb

WHILE THE VAMPIRES ENTERED THE HOUSE and appeared before our fear-lit eyes in disguise, creatures of another world paid us a visit in their true colors. They were the devils.

That is not possible, I'd shout to my people and sometimes to the little voices inside me. *God would not allow it!*

But the citizens murdered my conviction with their sharp glances. They told me I was only a kid. What did I know about things that belonged in hell! I still had to live life. Let them do the investigation. And they did. They investigated. They questioned their friends and neighbors. They quenched their curiosity with drops of anecdotes. There was the female, who begged a relative of ours to save her. *Save me,* the she-devil screamed. "She shouted, 'Nabafi,'" narrated our neighbor. "It means 'save me' in the Oromo language," our neighbor explained. There was the one that liked to visit the orphanage late at night and chase the girls during their short trips outside to the bathroom. The most recent appearance was granted to a woman who lived in our house. Satan was standing amid hundreds of buckets. The instant she made the sign of the cross and pronounced the name of God, both Satan and the buckets were gone.

The phenomenon of devils walking on the streets of Dire Dawa like citizens became more real as time passed by and people made it the center of their conversations. You would encounter Satan everywhere, day and night. Although I was very young and inclined to believe anything, I could not bring myself to believe people's narration about their adventurous encounter with God's cursed angel. My huge and white-bearded God was too great in my head, and anyone who opposed His will must have been defeated and long dead and gone. Then, one afternoon, I happened to be at my uncle's home, sitting outside on the stairs, talking over tea with my cousins, when suddenly, we heard my uncle screaming from inside. We all ran into the house. I was the last one to hallucinate the dark black figure with a large *gabi* wrapped around his shoulder. My uncle grabbed a cross from his room and waved it at Satan and shouted, *In the Name of the Father, the Son, and the Holy Spirit.* The banished angel disappeared into the house and my whole world was shattered, for Satan could not be true, and even if he was real, he could not be appearing like that in Christian people's house, as if he were a regular person. Wasn't it enough that he lived in my head, tempting me to disobey God and to sin every minute of the day! Now, he pretended to do that in person, where everything was much more convincing. No, all was inconceivable, and I refused to believe my eyes. No one could tell me what to make my convictions of and the devil existed not.

Allah Akbar—Allah Akbar, shouts a man with a prominent voice from a distant mosque throughout the day. Each time I hear the sound of those words, new neurons seem to come to life in my brain. And I too join the voice that's invading the city and chant *Allaahu Akbar,* unaware of the meaning, from my own mosque, built with bricks of hunger and steeples of solitude.

God is a ghostly presence in our house. He is in the giant fruitless trees, in the eye-witnessing walls, in the bloodstained ground, in the lizards-hosting ceiling. I'd see Him whenever I kneeled down on the floor by the bedside beside mom, my fingers intertwined, my eyes lifted up to the ceiling. I'd see Him through the walls late at night when a flock of shrieks and silences flew in from outside. I'd see Him in the hot stream vermilion that decorated our veranda on a regular basis at night.

The only Catholic church in town stands majestically a block away from our house, piggybacking a dormitory for the priest on the left wing and a convent/orphanage on the right wing. Every day, after mass, mom and I tour the entire church, stopping to visit and say a prayer to the statues of Virgin Mary (our interceptor), Sacred-Heart Jesus, and the crucified Jesus (our Savior), St. Anthony (mom's and my sister's favorite saint), St. Augustine (the patron of our church), and St. Theresa (the saint who lost her fingers because she looked at them and thought they were beautiful). Ever since mom told me about St. Theresa's unfortunate story, I dare not consider anything in my body beautiful. I don't want to have that part cut off like it happened to St. Theresa. I recite one Our Father, Hail Mary, and

Glory to each statue. Churchgoers admire and brag about my godliness so much that I start fantasizing about meeting the Virgin Mary like the shepherdesses in Portugal and at Lourdes. I imagine our encounter and how I would tell the believers about it and everyone's incredulity in hearing my incredible story.

The girls and the boys from the orphanage are the choir at church. They sing gospel, and many Catholics see them as a threat that will eventually extinguish the hymns and convert the church into a Pentecostal one. Except Sundays, when they dress up in their choir garb and sit in the choir section upstairs in the rear end of the church, the rest of the week, they occupy the front pews facing the altar. I usually sit with them, but, often, the Mother Superior catches me talking and grabs my ear to lead me to where mom is sitting. I say the mass all the way through and sing the hymns until my jaw hurts. The nun, who sits behind our row, a plump short old lay, always orders me to keep my voice down.

This is a mass, little girl. Not a screaming contest.
And whenever I scratch my head that itches from the lice, she slaps my hand. During the rosary recital, especially, being extremely bored, I catch a louse or its nit from the base of my hair and murder it using as a weapon the bottom nails of my two thumbs. I like the crushing sound that makes when I dash it between my fingers. But I have to pay my pleasure with a well-addressed slap on my hand and a threatening look from the old nun.

Mom leaves for the capital. She is dying, I think, and she is running to another city for help. People with the title "doctor," apparently, are believed to be saviors and could restore life to her. Or maybe she is simply out to experience peace, far away from this dungeon. I am staying at the orphanage. Next to the church. I am surrounded with Jesuses, Marys, wooden crosses, nuns, and priests. I thought that the only form of saving mom is interested in resided in heaven. *The body, Meti, the one in heaven is concerned solely with the soul; the one in Addis treats the body. There is a huge difference.* It's an excruciating life in here. It's an incessant experience of emotions. I am overwhelmed with guilt: I say a profane word and Jesus reproaches me from his cross. I am overwhelmed with solitude: the older girls entice me with the charms of their grown-up world but refuse to let me in. I try to be as obsequious as I can with words and self-deprecating behavior, and I half-succeed in making friends. But night is cruel. I get laughed at or I am pitied whenever I pee in bed, which happens every night. I blow my chance to be friends with the older girls, share secrets. And which secrets would I tell? I have none. I feel left out.

Blood follows me from our veranda to the orphanage. The girls whose world I am so anxious to step in hurry out of the church to create a circle around one of them. The lass is crying, and her friends' invasion has the purpose of transforming her state of mind, stifling the tears, comforting her sorrow. I can hear them speaking a set of words and terms I have never heard before. Blood is dribbling down on the floor, in the churchyard. Although I can't figure whose blood it exactly is, I suppose it must be coming from the girl who is desperately crying.

I ask, *What's going on? What's wrong with her? Why is she crying? What is this spot on the floor? Is it blood? Where is it coming from? Did somebody get hurt? Did she fall?*

No one is paying attention to me, let alone answering my annoying questions. I can just feel it is a secret they are keeping from me, and I reproach myself for being younger than those girls and for not understanding.

A bell rings at each meal, and the dinnertime bell is the one I am most familiar with. When I live at home and go to the orphanage to play, it is that ring that dictates the time for me to go home. Eating at the orphanage is all an adventure. Girls and boys devour each other to get more food on their plates. And if the food promises any palatability or sweets are at stake, the war is even fiercer. The voices crash against each other, making it impossible to hear one another. Then, the nun in charge yells at us to be quiet.

Let us rise and ask the Lord to bless our meal!

In unison, everyone makes the sign of the cross, says one Our Father, one Hail Mary, one Glory and concludes by asking, *Father, bless our meal, give bread to those who do not have any, bless the meal of those who don't remember to give Thee thanks, Amen.* The colliding voices are right back on, shouting, squealing, laughing, and again fighting for more food.

Shower is taken once a week. Saturday is the elected day of cleansing. We gather by the stalls and wait for our turn to taste the clean feeling of the water flowing on our skin. We get ready to transport the bucket filled with water to the stalls. We fill a mug and spill the water over our body and use one soap in common to scrub the dirt off.

Before going off to bed, we oil each other's hair, comb it, and then do braids. We are up late, talking.

When I grow up, I would like to fly.

You can't. You're going to be big and weigh much more than now, and it'll be hard.

Well, I can go to school and learn how to fly.

No school teaches you how to fly.

They do too. And if they don't, I'm going to build one.

How?

All I need is ask God for a bunch of wings. Once he provides me with the wings, it's a matter of knowing how to use them.

God isn't going to give you wings just like that. What do you think this is? God is not a vendor at the market.

Watch me! I will be either a student or a teacher at the School of Flying.

Be careful not to break your back on the way to insanity!

Since it's scary to walk to the restroom, located a few yards away from the bedrooms (with all the bad spirits around), we keep a bucket to pee in inside every room. But some nights, the buckets get full, and we are forced to use the bathroom. One night, on the way back to our room, the girls start screaming and running. I look around to see what is it that's making them run and I imagine I see a black figure, but it is blurry and seems so unreal. We all run inside our room.

The girls, breathlessly, say to each other, *Did you see it? That was him. Satan.*

Wow, he looks exactly like a man. How strange!

That is not strange. He is supposed to look like man.

You're right! He is a fallen angel. And angels look like us.

No, they don't. They're white and beautiful and have wings and can fly. We're black and ugly and have no wings and you've seen me how many times I've tried to fly from my bunk bed and fell.

That's because we're temporarily wingless and it's all Eve's fault.

Is that why Satan is walking free outside? Because he knows that we're temporarily wingless and couldn't fly to heaven to tell on him.

You're all so ignorant. Satan is here because he lives here.

No, he doesn't. He lives in hell.

Stupid! There is no such thing. He was banished from heaven the way we were banished from paradise. And you think God would have bothered in wasting his time to create two different places to punish sinners of the same kind.

Satan and man are not one kind.

You bet they are.

Then, why did you run away from him when you saw him earlier? Why are you scared of him if he is like you?

Because he is a grown-up and I am only a young calf.

I hate myself for not being big or smart enough to understand; for not being as convinced as they are. If they are so sure they saw Satan, why aren't I? Why am I so skeptical? What is it that impedes my eyes from seeing clearly and my mind and heart from believing? How long am I condemned to live in darkness?

I return home from the orphanage sadder than ever. I feel different, as if I were in someone else's body. Dad-non-dad comes home with a list of names for me to choose from.

Desta (Joy): Perhaps that will wipe that frown off of your face and store a smile back to those dead lips. By the way, if you insist on keeping that frown, you're going to look like the night's twin sister.

Selamawit (Peaceful): That way every time you say your name, you will be reminded of that which you deny the people around you. Really, Meti, we've no peace due to the new role you are determined to play.

Abeba (Flower): Watch it, though! Once we name you after a flower, you gotta live up to your name. No more walking around like a zombie. We have never heard of a dead little girl walking.

He and mom decided that a name change is necessary to exorcise the bad spirits from my being. It has been months since I've started acting devilish, so they have good reasons to think that I may have been possessed by the devil. I frown too often. I refuse to do what I'm told to do. I answer back to the heads of the house, thus breaking the "Honor thy father and thy mother . . ." commandment. I've kicked my classmate and friend out of our living room in the middle of doing homework and thrown her backpack after her. I hardly speak to anyone and spend my days locked in a room with my grown-up books and ripe thoughts. And no one can shake me or scare me out of my withdrawal, for so far oblivion is the only place where I feel safe and unscathed. The vampire throws all kinds of names in the air and laughs each time my big black eyes look at him bewildered and at the same time irritated. But mom isn't very good at laughing, so she hits me instead and bids me to change this attitude of mine or else. When mom sees my case to be hopeless, she takes me to one of those purifying holy lakes all the way to Addis Ababa. The place is so far away from being peaceful that even a devil-possessed kid like me can be frightened by it. A series of godly people lead us to the blessed lake and I am washed anew, born again like a Christian who's been enlightened with the idea of the grandeur of God's kingdom. But, of course, I am too young to comprehend all this.

Indeed, the thought that clouds my head is how all these people can be willing to wait on a queue just to be immersed in that dirty, cold water, in that cold city, during that cold season, and be baptized by a man who doesn't even have the decency to veil his cold eyes with some warmth.

Negotiations with the devil become more frequent. It is natural to bribe the spirit for an ounce of indulgence. Like adding one plus one, I am sure of the results. It is then that innocence is converted into bonds, a capital from which I profit coins for ice cream. So I stain my hands with steel blood. The incriminating evidence doesn't end here. I help my tongue into a firing of lies. I design strategies to manipulate the mind into performing its wicked ritual just in time before the guilt trips track start their engines. In the meanwhile, I listen intently to the priest's sermon. His eloquence in delivering the message from God of love and justice puts me under a spell each time. I listen to his words the same way one listens to the lyrics of a popular song. His message is always of the same nature: the road rules to the Kingdom, all about the stray corners, the rewards and the punishments. His words are more engraved in me than my mother's shouts to wash my vagina (bread she calls it: *dabo*), and my dirty feet. I turn my back on the fallen angel to start a new chapter of negotiations with God. But bargaining with Him isn't an easy job. It involves waiting and a fat chance of getting the request granted. For that which seems good to you now may result to be bad later. And who knows better than God? But I have no time for that. I want instant delivery. And I don't want to sacrifice more things than life has already denied me. Fuck abstinence! I shall indulge every whim that dares to cross my head.

Book 2

Exodus of Souls

T HE DAMAGE WAS DONE. There was no mettle left to squeeze out of the reservoir of hope or faith, or whatever else life availed for its living creatures to hold on to. He had finished with their lives. Nearly forty people were disentangled from the strings that had attached them to this world. From now on, their presence would no longer affect the environment. Their bodies would exist no more. All the hardships, the heartaches, the burdens, seemingly, were of no use. Life showed no gratitude.

Denizens gathered about outside my house, screwing and widening their big eyes, stooping, feeding their hungry curiosity with other people's no longer existing lives. I had just returned from school, and the overly excited, nosy crowd invading my street delayed my ingress into the safety net. I made my way past the shocked faces and the unintelligible tongues. As I reached the edge of the street, which fancied a downward slope, and faced the enormous, futile field that shouldered my house, which for the occasion exhibited dug holes and dead bodies, the end of the world flashed before my eyes. The earth was bare and still. I was trembling. I turned around and waded my way to the back, far away from reality. I singled myself out and took a stand where no one could see me but I could see everyone: the whole world on the palm of my mind. I resolved to stay one moment longer. My small stature gave the impression of enveloping the rest of the throng. I could not move for something had taken hold of me; something hard had grown within me at that very moment. My hands pushed the heavy door in, and I persuaded my legs to step inside the house and shut the outside behind me. No tear was released to extract the mass that had just piled up within. The house was empty. Everyone was out surely to satisfy his or her thirsty mind about the latest news. Who was to judge? Certainly not I. I was not to open my mouth. I would put this whole thing aside; let it take its course and segue into the realm of oblivion.

Oh, Goodness Lord! And to think that my son could have been one among those corpses, said mom, choking in her voice. *Yet, God is merciful and once again he spared me my son's life.*

The melancholy in her eyes and her rigid countenance were more visible than usual. She had spent the entire night awake and I with her. A loud shriek had echoed all the way to our living room/bedroom, soliciting her to lose heart. She ran across the room and out of the house, in the meantime, I was sure, negotiating with the Almighty for her wild son's safe return home. Oh, the power of faith and prayer! He and his friends had crossed that futile field, met the life taker (the evil one on earth, not the bountiful one above), and conversed with him and come home safe. Some people would have called it luck, others fate. Mom thought of the miraculous occurrence as an answer to her prayers. I, for my part, thought nothing and suffered in that ignorance to which a child is held captive.

As it was the routine, mom and I went to church that afternoon. I had hoped that the confusion and invasion on our lot would have hindered our visit to God's House for once. But my hopes were groundless. One had to walk over mom's cadaver first in order to make her miss church. She had a way with life. She held her head up no matter what, and her principal rules were: Reprioritize God! Say your prayer! And keep quiet! I was brought up by that law. But that evening at church, I entertained myself with a train of thought that belonged to my new secret life. My mind was pregnant with novel pleasant ideas. I conceived the world to be a garden, a park full of laughing children and joyous adults. I created new characters and gave them familiar faces. Or I took those familiar faces and imbued them with kindness. I was lost in reverie until mom held my hand to address Jesus' prayer "Our Father" to our Father and woke me up at once.

The Sunday sermon must have consisted mostly of the barbarous deed committed by man upon men. How that atrocious act of murder manifested the brutality and inhumanity in the character of man. How God must be deeply offended and hurt each time that type of atrocity occurred: He giveth life, He shall take it away. The audience must have been hanging to the priest's words and I, dissecting them, objecting his forcefulness in presenting them.

Let us pray for those who are no longer among us. Let us plead with our Fa-

ther to take them in His powerful embrace and grant them the entrance into His Kingdom. And to that man whose soul is obviously lost, let us pray that God may lead his way back home; that he may be forgiven for God's mercy is boundless and forgives all those who are deeply repented. Let us rise!

The priest concluded his monologue and let the crowd join him in a prayer.

For several weeks, the incident of the man who cold-bloodedly murdered nearly forty people and buried them in the dry underbridge beside my house was the center of most people's conversations in town. Denizens bragged about their testimony of horror at the sight of the crime site. They spoke of such a delicate matter as freely as a critic would summarize the plot of the latest movie. I dared not wonder aloud at their demeanor or question my aloofness, which increased at the rise of the pitch of their voice. I receded into distant lands and scratched at the depth of greater worlds, reaching higher levels with the aid of my imagination.

5

Darkness

(Only Members Allowed!)

Stretch out your hand toward the sky,
that over the land of Egypt
there may be such intense darkness that one can feel it.

Exodus 10:21

My family's problem has no name, no label to it. It just has a dance of its own, and it takes advantage of the wild night to display its choreography. One Two Three—Cha Cha Cha! I try hard to keep up with the steps, make the turns at the right time, detach my feet from the ground at the right degree, and land back on the floor with poise and grace. I am learning the dance, and I ask mom if she wishes me to teach her the steps, if she wishes me to practice with her, to give her my secret, the secret of my rhythm. But she waves my offer away. She'd rather watch me dance my way out of the wild night. As for her, life has ceased to be ever since the night began, and learning to dance would be trying to defeat death and who has strength for that.

The vampires visit our house religiously. Some come in the form of a stepfather. Some as police officers. Some as civilians. Some as customers in mom's squalid food shop. And the list goes on. My eyes learn to be wary. I look at everyone with a degree of suspicion. It is required of me: to suspect and to inspect. I observe everyone with a small amount of judgment. It is required of me: to form an opinion. Everyone seems to have a badge that reads: "I am here to hurt you." I ask why, not in so many words, only with a long-sustained, prying stare. But they won't answer. They only pat my head, pour out a condescending smile. They don't know that I am going to find a way to read their thoughts once they're gone. I am going to lie on my bed and lay out every note of their words and every pitch of their demeanor. They don't know that they will be held up to be dissected and eventually condemned, discarded. The church says that my actions are unhealthy. But lately, even the priests are starting to join the party of vampires on my list, so why trust their words? So I make up my mind to be the architect of my acts. No one else can influence me. No Spiritual Adviser. No Savior. No Parent. I will be my own guide. I will teach myself more elaborate steps of this complicated dance. And I will dance my way out of this wild wild night.

The night routine is everyday the same at home. Dinner, wash-up, listen to mom's gin-drinking clients' jokes, laugh, pray, sleep, and then chaos. Mom wanders in the house, waking up abruptly at the sound of a shriek or a gunshot! My son, she worries, and hurries outside in her *dirya,* a stick in the hold of her hand. And I watch her from a distance, with knots in my throat and goosebumps throughout my skin. She is my hero. Tall and dark; her hair usually parted in four plaits. And we stay outside, waiting under the veil of the lightless night, she in company of her prayers, which redound around the glowing rosary that she holds tight in her hands; and I in company of fear and fear and again fear. Fear that a thief will slice my mother's throat, mistaking the rosary beads for a jewel; fear that someone will show up in front of our door, bleeding, claiming justice, or worse yet cursing at mom; fear that the vampire we keep in the house will wake up and start a riot, in addition to the one that already exists in our hearts at that moment; fear that my brother won't show up and that the next day my mother and I will have to go search for his name amid the names or faces of scapegoats inside that awful place named prison.

Most memories come to me in the form of splintered glasses: in pieces and edgy. They are like a live nightmare. It's funny to rewind the memory tape because right before facing Gehenna, mom and I get on our knees and plead with God to protect us in our sleep. And the haunting starts.

A woman is screaming. She is bearing a deep cut somewhere on her head from where blood is gushing. Oh Lord Have Mercy on Us! Did the crazy, crazy prince do that? Some men just walked in the house. Oh mother, what're you doing? Getting out of the bed, fishing the wooden stick from under the bed and going to dare the covetous night owls. Oh My Heart Be Still! Just missed them. Thank Thee, God! Are those people talking? Are those voices real or do they belong to the dream? My darling father-non-father holding a gun to my brother's head? The police. Oh, the police! How come the hostage is the one who's being handcuffed and carried away? Police. Does that mean we need to get back to pay those terrifying visits in jail? Jail. Oh, jail is much better and closer than the other abode. Oh, Heaven Forbid! The other place is way too far away and petrifying. How many hours to get there? And by foot. Under that fiery sun. Oh, Poor Mother, how many years to heal? Someone is walking back and forth down our courtyard. He is holding a rifle. Is it the police? Is it He-Vampire's younger brother? The flickering light. Mother, stop peeping through the curtains! Let me see. Is that darling father-non-father in his vampire role? Blackout—the telephone is ringing. The insults. How long has it been? How many years? Is that the prince on the line calling all the way from outer space to insult mom for marrying a monster? How dare he? What a crying shame! My grandmother died. Why am I here, in this house, all by myself holding to the veranda door? Crying. It is deep night. Did she have to die at night? Oh, Darkness, Please Give Me a Break!

It is deep night and I am sitting in our courtyard, across from the living room, bawling my eyes out. Mom endeavors to calm me, but her crying is keeping her almost as busy as I. My stepfather is holding a rope in his hand, and he is saying time and again that he's going to hang himself. He's pacing the court back and forth, looking for a perfect suicide spot. The trees look quite right. But maybe not. I beg him to please not kill himself, to please stay with me and live forever. He is not listening. He walks in the house, down the veranda, to the kitchen. I follow him for I fear his not coming back. I fear my losing him. He may be a vampire at night, but when the dawn breaks and the rays of sun sift through our window, he restores back to me every drop of blood he sucks from my soul in the darkness. I don't want to lose him. I don't ever want to renounce to those magical moments with him in the bars, he drinking his beloved beer, I my beloved Coke. Our moments at the car terminal, getting passengers on his car, my jewel. Our moments after school with me sitting on his bed giving an account of the fun and unpleasant moments at school. No, not him! My hero and king of the daytime. He grabs a knife from one of the drawers, and then he walks over to the refrigerator and cuts a big piece of raw meat. He gets some *berbere* and pours Ethiopian, homemade honey wine in a mug and goes back to the courtyard. His car is parked behind the living room. He gets in the driver seat and makes himself comfortable. My crying gets louder, for I am confused and I don't understand what's going on. What do a knife, raw meat, hot pepper, and wine symbolize? He cuts the meat in smaller slices and dips each piece in the *berbere*. He is eating and helping his bite wash down with a mouthful of wine, and he's laughing heartily like a person who's just heard a brilliant joke.

⸴   ⸴   ⸴

I wake up in the middle of the night and find mom standing by the window, peeping through the curtain. I force my eyes open and, without moving from the bed, I ask mom what is she looking at.

This man gets crazier everyday.

I tell her to let the man be crazy and come back to sleep. She doesn't answer me. I get up and join mom by the window and take a peek myself. A man is standing in the middle of our courtyard, holding a rifle, like a soldier. Another man is walking up and down the court and once and then comes to peep in our room through the same window we're using to spy on him. His figure in the darkness is like that of a phantom, scary and unreal.

The living room door is ajar. Notwithstanding the uproar of the small crowd outside, I must have stayed asleep. But the loud shriek of a woman makes me jump out of the bed. I peep through the slightly open door, and I see mom on her knees, begging the vampire, who's holding a gun to my brother's head, to spare her son's life. I look at my brother's face, and he shows no sign of reaction or anger or fear. He has the look of someone who has given up the fight for survival. On the other hand, the vampire's face shows zeal, ambition to live and destroy and win and rule. There are other people I don't care to acknowledge. And I don't dare to go any farther from the room because something in my body holds me back. Some relentless thing in my body hinders me from taking any step forward. The police arrive and take my brother away. Mom bows to the floor and cries out of desperation.

Fists are being thrown heedlessly at the face that belongs to a young man named Ard. The crush of the hand against the skull has the sound of thunder. I run out of my bed to the veranda and pull the fist blower out of my way. The broken reed falls on the floor. Blood is gushing out of his head and face and running down our veranda. I get down on my knees, shaking like a leaf in the wind. Gently, I lift the tortured skull and let it lean on my lap, and I put my hands around the fainted young man's chest. His lips and nose and eyes look like an abstract painting portrait on which the facial features are displaced on purpose for artistic reasons. A Picasso masterpiece. Mom is sitting on the floor by the living room door. Her eyes are wide open and directed to the sky, her hands thrown carelessly on the floor, her head leaning vertically against the wall. She gives the impression of someone who has been crucified while sitting. She is crying and mumbling unintelligible words, which I could swear, are referred to God. The darkness in the atmosphere makes everything more intense, and even the grip of my hand over that body feels like lifting a hundred tons of weight. My pajama and my hands and my bare feet are wet with blood. And I am feeling excruciating pain and I am crying and I am shouting at the vampire, *What kind of person are you? What kind—ah—ah—ah? Look just what you did! Loooook!*

A young woman is standing outside our door, crying, her hands holding the wound on her head. She is complaining and pointing fingers, and I don't understand why she's come to mom. To my bigger astonishment, mom gets on her knees and asks the stranger for forgiveness. *It's the alcohol—a good heart—an angel—a prince.* The two women exchange a set of phrases I can't understand and cry a duet. I too start to cry because I don't know what else to do, and seeing mom get on her knees in front of some drunk woman to make amends for what some other drunk, crazy young men did just breaks my heart. Blood keeps oozing out of the cut and, in contrast with the darkness, its color turns like that of wild berries. The bleeding girl leaves, and mom gets on her knees to make negotiation with God.

The house is on fire. Smoke is invading the entire place, and the stifling smell has gotten past the walls to wake us up. Mom somehow figures the origin from where the fire started. She, and I after her, run to the basement, which is located underneath what used to be garage. We descend the stairs. Mom kicks the door open, and the flames almost blind her sight. She bids me to stay away from there and goes out in the neighborhood to look for help. My best friend Reuben's mother comes in aid. The two of them run to the fire department and, by the time they come back, the basement is entirely ablaze. Since they can't get in from the door because of the fire, the firefighters go to the back of the fortress, on the empty underbridge, tear one part of the wall down, and extinguish the blazes. The entire house is invaded by policemen and guns and rifles—rifles, guns and policemen, and ashes and smoke. . . .

Oh, God Almighty Omnipotent! cries mom.

Mom has gone nuts, and she's desperately trying to get her outcry across to God. The princes have gone to sleep beside hyenas on the dry underbridge. The vampires too have gone crazy and are readying their sharp teeth for the nightly bite.

Voices explode like bombs, *I want this whole situation to be over with. I want all of us dead, dead, dead.*

Fingers are pointing, *Take this outlaw, criminal away.*

Hearts are breaking. Minds are losing reason. Mom reaches the depths of pain and sorrow. She weeps and moans and gives it all to God.

Some men break in our house. Brand-new vampires. They go straight to the kitchen and turn the light on. Mom and I watch them through the slightly open door from the living room. I push mom aside and carefully close and lock the living room door.

I tell mom, *We should get back to sleep.*

You go back to sleep.

She finds a big stick somewhere in the room, fixes it tight and well in the hold of her hand, and walks toward the door.

Are you going to fight the thief?

She orders me to go back to sleep.

Mom, please, don't go. He has a knife. All thieves have knives. He's gonna kill you. Please, don't go fight that thief.

She tells me to keep quiet and not to worry because she has God by her side; therefore, nothing will happen to her. She opens the door slowly, and my heart comes out of my chest. She takes a step out of the living room and I resolve to go after her, but it's too late for her to play heroine. The men were through with their mission, whatever that was, and have already left the house. I sigh with relief. Mom goes out of the house to see if she can catch up with them.

Mom's body is being dragged on the floor, her hands clinging to the prince's leg. The police is taking him away, and she is imploring them not to. She screams she won't let go of him. As usual, she's using her tears and her desperate motherly cry to change those men's mind, but her effort is in vain. The entire government and police are corrupt, and the vampire has all of them in the palm of his hands. They handcuff the prince and take him away. Mom remains on the floor, puts her arms around a tree, and cries. He-Vampire stands a few feet away, indifferent to mom's deep sorrow.

I yell at him, *Why are you doing this to the prince? And to my mother? Why? Why? Why?*

He doesn't answer me and walks away. I hug mom and hold her tight against me and assure her that it's all going to be all right; that tomorrow we will go to the detention center and get him back. But she's too deep in her suffering to be consoled with my words. She knows more than I do how life works.

He-Vampire gives me a paper with a written statement on it and asks me to sign it.

I ask, *What is it about?*

It says that the prince attempted to kill me last night.

I'm not going to sign it because I didn't see or hear the prince doing any of that.

He bids me to be a good girl and sign that damn paper.

I won't because I don't believe the prince did nothing at all last night or ever. And even if he had, I wouldn't sign anything against him. For God's sake, he's a prince.

He shouts at me that I am just a brat and a bad, bad little girl. *Very bad, bad girl.* And never to talk to him again unless it is to tell him that I've decided to sign that paper. And my heart breaks because I know I am never going to turn the prince in and that means to renounce to my dad-non-dad and that is painful.

The banging on our window is louder than the crowing of the roosters in the morning, kookoolookooo . . . (our alarm clock). He-Vampire's alcohol-driven words emerge from his mouth like drizzles of rain, slow and inarticulate. He tells me that he knew about an Arab who sold the child he had adopted to the real father for seventeen thousand *bir.* He yells that he's going to sell me to my real father and make a lot of money off me.

I am gonna sell you, he yells over and over.

I blame the ridicule and insincerity of his words on alcohol, for he's my only father. It's his first name that I carry as my last name. What is he talking about?

Sell you, he yells, *That's what I'm going to do. I'm sure I'll make a fortune. Damn it! After all, it's your father. He must be willing to pay a large amount of money to buy his daughter. Unless, ha, ha, ha, ha—*

I tell mom, *That man is crazy, emaye.*

I get off the bed, turn the stereo on, and blast the music. I pop into the bed beside mom and I tell her, *Now, we can sleep in peace.*

The prince is imprisoned for more than three months. He is falsely accused of imposture. He-Vampire reported to the police that the prince wandered the city, disguised under many identities, rendering himself unrecognizable by travestying in different costumes and wigs. I can't understand which part of that charge is a crime that deserved three months of jail. Moreover, no evidence or the benefit of a trial was given. Mom and I go to pay the prince a visit once a week, usually on Sunday afternoons. The prison is in the middle of nowhere, and we have to walk for hours to get there. Mom prepares food to take to him, pouring her heart and soul into the meal. We start our journey as soon as she finishes packing provisions for more than one prisoner. She is sadder than ever during that long walk to the gated house and answers in syllables to anything I say. I suppose she's too busy either praying or wondering about her prince's circumstances and why in God's name he is in prison for something he did not do.

I am sitting on the stairs that lead to the basement, preparing our made-of-fabric house and mud-meals. My friends haven't gotten home yet, so I am anticipating their arrival. Instead, Ard, mom's gin-drinking client and the vampire's victim whose bleeding tortured skull I once held in my arms, approaches my nomadic site.

I tell him, smiling, *I am getting ready before the rest of the crew comes in.*
He smiles back and says, *We can start playing until the others come.*
Me and you?
Yeah!
But you're big. You're a real grown-up.
So I'll make a better play grown-up, he insists.
I surrender and say, *OK.*
I go over his tasks in the house. He gets real close to me and touches parts of me I feel ashamed he's touching and, somewhere deep inside, my most private part reacts to the touching. And, suddenly, I have the awareness that that kind of touching is a sin. I swerve swiftly and tell him, *I don't feel comfortable.* He stands up nervously and says that he didn't mean to scare me, that he just wanted to play husband and wife. I tell him, *Leave me alone. I want to play by myself. Just go, go, go!*

The prince, who by now lives in outer space, is home to see mom after three years of absence. He's brought a woman with him. Since the prince is celebrating his return with his friends on an everyday basis, his girlfriend spends most of her time with me. She takes me with her shopping, for dinner by candlelight, and to the movies, which seem to air solely Indian musicals, with the women lamenting over their impossible loves in their high-

pitched voices. I am very happy because I've never been to the movies before. The only giant screen I've ever been exposed to was in the conference
room at church, to watch religious films. And even though the soprano-
voice Indian women and their baritone- and tenor-voice men tire me
after a while, these movies drag me away from my routine. And I like to
spend my days with the prince's vacation woman, for she turn heads of the
entire race of men in town.

The heartthrob and I are in the bathroom. She's taking a shower, and I
am sitting on a wooden stool by the door, watching her pour clear water
on her plain, dark-chocolate body. Suddenly, I see blood flooding the
floor. She doesn't give me time to be scared because she starts jumping
on the wet floor and she's grinning and shouting with joy. She stoops to
hug me. I'm confused. I don't see what's so joyous about a stream of blood
floating above the ground. All the other times that I saw blood, I also witnessed suffering and crying, especially crying. The girl at the orphanage
almost choked with tears as the blood dribbled on the floor in the churchyard. And the times blood ran down our veranda, somebody's skull, forehead, or nose was cracked open. Blood is evil. And here she is, this crazy,
extraterrestrial woman, exhilarated over the sight of her own blood. Is it
her own? Must be, unless it leaked somewhere from the bathroom. Soon,
she stops the train of my fighting thoughts and tells me that she's not going to have a baby after all. She repeats that she's not going to have the
prince's baby after all. She says she hasn't bled in a while and was preoccu-
pied that she might be having a baby. She tells me that she and I have to
celebrate this moment. She'll take me out. I listen to her without understanding. I can't possibly perceive what blood has to do with not having a
baby. And what need is there to celebrate this moment when blood is all
over the floor and her feet dipped deep into it?

The police are back to invade our veranda. He-Vampire is once again
pointing fingers at the prince.

*He broke the nightstand and stole money, and tried to kill my brother with
a spear while he was sleeping; he took all the documents I received from the
Mengst for all the years I served my country and the revolution and burned
them; he's gonna kill both his mother and I with a knife, take him away immediately from this country. I want you to banish him from Ethiopia.*

The police handcuff the prince and, when mom shouts that he is innocent, He-Vampire throws her to the floor and says, *Arrest her, too.*

I shout, *Emaye,* and throw myself on top of her.

The prince is taken away. He is detained for a few days. When he gets released, the vampire brings from the immigration an order that requires the prince's immediate return to outer space.

Run, Meti, run, the prince's girlfriend says to me. Darkness has fallen upon my city, and the silence is reigning over the empty streets, which deafening sound pierces through my ears.

Faster, Meti, or they will catch us, she repeats.

I run after her, crying the question, *What have we done?*

Quiet, Meti, you'll have us killed. We're already past the curfew.

What's a curfew? I ask, though the word is very familiar, since I read it in one of the fairytales included in the book that I lost my virginity to at the age of five. But this picture doesn't quite fit that of Cinderella hurrying home after stealing the prince's heart.

What's a curfew? I ask again.

She doesn't answer my question. I can perceive fear all over her body and her demeanor. There is a trembling look about her face, as if her teeth are squeaking from coldness. We have just left the movie theater, where we bawled our eyes watching Bollywood movies. We are so far from home, I don't even want to think about running that distance.

I don't feel like running, I complain.

Don't be a child, Meti. This is serious. They'll shoot us if they find us out on the streets at this hour.

You still haven't told me what a curfew is.

I just did. We can't be out here at this time of the night. We shouldn't have gone to the movies so far.

But why? What's wrong with being out so late?

Go ask Mengestu that. Oh, God, what things you have me saying, Meti. You'll have us both shot.

I project in my ears the sound of a gunshot and then visualize the bullets piercing her heart first and then mine, causing our falling to the ground in slow motion, and welcoming death. God, run, Meti, run, I think to myself and keep up the pace with my movie buddy, whose body language is presently saying that at the moment nothing matters more than saving her life.

The next day I ask mom more information on curfew and why couldn't we stay out on the streets after dusk. *Oh, Lord, who put these ideas in your head, now? Don't worry about any of that. It doesn't concern you. What you should mind is the fact that after 7 P.M., you have no business fumbling around the streets. How many times did I tell you that before?* Mom goes on and on. It's a miracle that I didn't get a whipping last night. But the severe look that she wears on her face and the reproachful tone of her voice make up for any missed punishment.

My dry throat-like mind is killing me for a glass of knowledge, so I ask mom to give me some details on Mengestu Hailemariam. She gives me a taste of her assassin look, instead.

Mom, was Haile Selassie a better leader than Mengestu?

Silence is once again her response.

Is it true that Mengestu choked Haile Selassie to death while he was sleeping?

Mom is doing as much threatening as she can without the use of words.

That they put a pillow on his face until he stopped breathing? That he is buried underneath our president's bed?

My questions enrage mom so much that I have to read the answer in her eyes and walk away or else. I'll have to find out elsewhere about the curfew and our extremely nationalist, Communist president and our internationally acclaimed deceased king. But what corrodes my head the most are the questions to which the answers are not present in books. What is it that obliges mom to silence and to live with that everlasting somber look on her face? Why is it that the prince tells me he'll send me to Castro if I behave badly? Who is Castro? And what kind of name is Castro?

6

Entrée

If you do not seal the holes,
You will have to rebuild the walls.

Swahili proverb

MOM IS NOT IN THE ROOM. I can still feel her near me, yet I know she is not in the room. What to do with myself? Shall I persuade my thoughts to silence and befriend the lizards that are walking up these walls? If I go outside I could even attract the attention of the stray cats that my mother feeds, our two dogs, and my brother's mischievous monkey (oh, do I hate that monkey). It's a beautiful day. Everyday is a beautiful day in Dire. God seems to enjoy giving bread to those who lack teeth. What am I to do with a beautiful day? What is any of us here to do with a beautiful day? Do people die often? As often as the sky falls and shatters into this heart of mine. It tastes so bitter to digest this sour life. I have empty spaces lying beside me thoughts raping the tranquility of a sea pains turning into wounds tears flooding into pools. Cry. Suit yourself. Alone in this empty room making conversations with fire burning every inch of soul if soul is called the life within if soul called the life without the throat that chokes at ugliness outside I roam and always will this place inside too chilly to be in better gather the seeds too soon then leave this site still waiting to bloom . . . Suit yourself and burn! Burn till you can no more. Burn because burning is all good or bad alive present true real burn of pain burn of joy just make sure you burn always and forever.

I sit in Hajji's spacious hallway, chatting with a relative of Hajji's who's my age and just moved into the house. Ahiram, Hajji's son, is a few feet away from us, washing his feet and other parts of his body, readying for prayer. People are smoking hookah and hashish in the room behind us.

You know, your father is a Muslim, announces the angel.

I ask her what is she talking about.

Don't tell me you don't know that the vampire isn't your father?

My proud and hurt self says, *Of course, I do.*

Then, you should also know that your real father is a Muslim.

I am already repelled by the idea of having a different father from the one I have and if that real father doesn't even belong to the True Faith, then, what's the use of being born at all?

You're wrong. My father is not a Muslim. I can guarantee you that.

She slaps my guarantee with an all-knowing laugh and starts talking with Ahiram in Somali. I can't understand a word they're saying, but she gets back to me and says, *See, everybody knows.*

She asks Ahiram in Amharic, *Isn't Meti's real father a Muslim?*

He replies in Somali and there goes again the blankness over the darkness in my head.

You see, he's speaking in Somali because he doesn't want you to hear the truth. But Wallahi, Meti! Your father is Muslim.

I leave Hajji's with darkness so vast within me that if someone broke my soul open, he would have been stricken dead. I go straight to Miriam, my second mom, who's making *injera* in the small room by mom's garden. I sit on a chair and I ask her if I have a real father and if I do, is he a Muslim.

She laughs at my naiveté, I suppose, and then tells me, *Enat Ghela* (that's what she calls me), *it's true, you have another father and you know that* (I'm not sure if by that she means that I am the queen of denials or that my father's many appearances on our veranda and his legendary disappearing acts, especially the final one, are meant to be real in my head), *but he's certainly not a Muslim. I can assure you on that,* she concludes.

I don't know what to do with all these assurances; one assuring me my father's a Muslim, the other assuring me the contrary. The darkness in my head and my heart and soul grows vaster and vaster. I trust more Miriam's words because her countenance when she uttered the answer to my question wasn't mocking at all, which in the case of the angel who announced the identity of my paternity lineage was.

Mom shouts, *It's time to go to church.*

Her voice feels like thunder in my ears. I force myself to extract from my being every echo of that voice, for it's driving me crazy. I join mom in our living room/bedroom and sit on the old couch and watch her change into decent clothes in the honor of the House of God. I watch painstakingly her large-sized breasts and dark-chocolate skin adhered to that tall body and I imagine how that real father of mine wandered his paw on her, his claws scratching her back like the man next door does to his girlfriend. She's speaking to me but I can't hear anything she's saying, for my mind is too busy thinking the worst about her. My body is stiff on the couch and I can't bring it to move. My heart makes room to open a saving account for grudge. How could she have done that with a man and still act like a saint! Oh, did I think mom was a saint! All her churchgoing and godly preaching seem hypocritical now. Vermiculate thought processes stream in my head, as the darkness fills me thoroughly, leaving no access to a shed of light.

My father's appearances and disappearing acts are more real in my head than the abstractions of dreams are in my sleep. I can see him in his colonel uniform, standing on the verandah, stooping to kiss me goodbye. I can see him sitting with us on Sunday afternoons, listening to the radio. But nowadays everything seems unreal in that house. The vampires, the police, the guns, the blood, and even mom. And something tells me that I am required to keep everything that is related to my father a secret, like I always have. Especially now that everyone seems to know more than I thought they did about my father. I want to ask mom why my father is a secret. I want to ask her why he was taken away from us. I want to ask her why I have two fathers and how come one of them, the one I love the most, likes blood and nights. I want to ask her why an ordinary man who makes a living by driving people from one city to the next has the power to influence the police, the judges, and those who decide whether someone deserves banishment from the country. I want to ask her why the police won't leave us alone. And why she has to turn to attorneys for help if they are the worst of sinners. I want to ask her what is the content of all those pages that she asks me to read for her, every day, or all the paperwork she asks me to fill out and the letters she asks me to write and sign by the pseudonym *the historian*. Why does she call herself the historian?

My father's disappearing acts are not going to remain to be the only legend in the house of ghosts, vampires, and saints. Two relatives of mom are on their way to be banished. The first one accompanies mom to church early in the morning and offers his manly chest to take the bullets in place of mom whenever the occasion presents. The second victim is Putiel, the man who taught me how to read at a precocious age. But neither of them is going to be spared for his contribution to the utilitarianism movement for protecting a helpless woman or teaching a child how to read. But for now their unverifiable disappearance is on hold. It is the turn of mom's gin-drinking client, my math tutor. Suddenly, he stops showing up on our veranda to get his nightly pint and to explain to me the marriages between numbers. I ask mom where my friend is. I want to know if his disappearance has anything to do with the blood that oozed out of his lip a few nights earlier, when the police dragged his body outside from our house. I know that happens all the time in our house but could it be that he too will disappear like my father did? Mom bids me stop asking questions. I insist on knowing what happened to my grown-up friend. I am pregnant with a novel idea and ask mom if by any chance we could look him up on the list of the prisoners. She can't understand what I mean by that, and neither do I. But, one afternoon, she packs a meal enough for more than three people and bids me to follow her. I know from experience the time is visiting time in jail and the food mom carries with her just confirms my suspicion. I leap with joy when we get to the barred cell and my friend and tutor smiles at me and he thanks mom for the visit and the food. He asks me how my math is coming along and how is everyone doing. Are the boys busting my chops as always with their incredible, alcohol-driven jokes? I only smile back at him, and wonder why people live today as if yesterday never happened. He is arrested for doing nothing except sitting, laughing, and enjoying himself, and he accepts the injustice, delivering a series of smiles and thank yous to us. Why should he thank anybody at all, including those who bring him food, if they can't lift a finger to help him? I cry, and mom tells me I know better not to do that, especially here. I wipe my tears and tell mom I want to go home. My sequestered friend holds my hand and makes me promise that I'll be a good girl. Instead, I cry for days until months pass and erase his image from my head.

It's night and mom and I are on the train on our way to Addis Ababa, the capital. I don't know what we're escaping from, but something in our sudden departure and mom's restless countenance reveals to me that we are fugitives. The train shakes like a smoothie blender. Mom grabs me, and we cringe under the seat. She tells me to pray, *God hears better children's prayers.* I beg God to please let us live. I promise Him that I'll light as many candles I can't count if he makes the train OK. But some whisperers slur about the presence of a bomb between the rail tracks. Mom tells me, *Pray!* I assume my prayer has gotten to God's ears for we're back on our seats, alive, and the train, whole, with its motor running fine. Now, I have to think

whether I'll have to light the candles in Addis or is it all right if I wait until we go back to Dire?

In Addis, we tarry at one of our close relatives' house. Pallu is married
to a wealthy man, Shupham. He breeds cows and sells the milk and that
must bring him a lot of money because whenever he comes to Dire, de-
spite mom's invitation to stay with us, he takes a room in the most presti-
gious hotels in town. I am happy here because it's a different routine. Early
in the morning, Shupham and his foremen load the track with hundreds
of gallons of milk. Then, Shupham, his son, Hupham, and I drive to the
city to distribute milk to various locations. And that gives me joy and peace.
But joy and peace are to be smothered soon. One evening, I get back home
from my daily excursion out in the city and find mom and Hupham's sister sitting in the bedroom open-mouthed. They tell me how Imnah, the
youngest child, found her father's gun, took it over to the cow-breeder,
and ordered him to pull the trigger. The poor man, who's from the country and doesn't have a clue about guns, shot.

Mom, still open-mouthed, says, *Thank God, the bullet flew skyward and
no one got hurt.*

After a long sojourn in the capital, we're headed back to Dire. The train on
which mom and I are traveling gets broken, or at least that is what I assume, and it stops for days in the middle of nowhere. Mom begins recit-
ing the rosary in silence, and I promise God another series of candles if
He guarantees us a safe return home. The men who are sharing the compartment with us are very jolly and festive. Here we are train-wrecked and
these aliens are singing love and patriotic songs, dancing, making jokes
and laughing, turning that small, few-square-foot abode into a compartment of mirth. I can't help laughing at their jokes and silly talks because
their mirth is irresistibly contagious. They even make mom laugh, and
that's a revelation that these people have magic, for I know for a fact that
life has denied mom the gift of laughter. Mom laughs, the rosary tight between her fingers. I laugh, my mind free from dark streets. The jolly men
buy food in abundance and spread a variety of goods before my hungry
eyes and I'm suddenly pregnant with the idea that the possession of money
is at the root of the mirth of those people. I watch them extract the crispy,
worthy bills from their wallets, and I dream of the day we too will have
that kind of money. Then, I know we'd be able to buy not only mirth but
also peace, rest and placid sleep. . . . A vampire interrupts the stream of my

wishful thinking by appearing out of nowhere in our compartment. He sits beside mom, and the smile that life seemed to have granted her just a moment ago is wiped off. I am happy to see him, but soon I have to reproach myself for that because his appearance has destroyed mom's laughter and that just isn't fair so I blame life for it all. The smile isn't yet wiped off my face, for I'm intoxicated with mirth from these perfect strangers. But my mind is no longer free from the vision of dark streets. I find myself entering those same dark corners, a wonder dangling in my head: How in the world did he run into us amid so many departing trains and thousands of passengers? Isn't destiny a trip!

I am staying over at a relative's house for reasons unknown to me. Mom is back in Addis Ababa. Then, one ordinary afternoon, Miriam comes to get me. She announces with a big smile on her face, *Enat Ghela, you're leaving for Italy.*

I ask, *Italy, but why?*

You should be happy.

Happy, what for?

I have a tendency to stutter when I speak and she smiles at that, but her eyes are filled with tears. She holds my hand and we walk the hours-long walk.

Gash Putiel, who years earlier played the role of maestro in my beginning phase of reading, tries to persuade me to choose Italy over Ethiopia.

He says, *Think about it, Meti! You won't have to deal anymore with Judah and the rest of the neighborhood kids. They will no longer bother you if you go to Italy.*

I object, *They're not that bad. I prefer to be called names by them than leave.*

You gotta be kidding me. Just remember the times you came home crying because they made fun of you or wanted to fight with you.

It's OK, I insist.

Miriam says, *Enat Ghela, it's better this way.* And she cries and walks away.

I demand, *I want to say goodbye to my friends.*

Everyone says, *No way.*

Yes, way!

Meti, now, be a good girl and do what you're told to do.

I cry, *But I have to say goodbye to my friends; at least, to Reuben and Beriah and Jashab and Amram and Hajji's household and the girls at the orphanage and my classmates and my cousins and mom's gin-drinking clients and my brother's friends and* . . .

They interrupt my list and say, *Meti, Meti, Meti, listen carefully! This is serious. You cannot bid farewell to anybody. You're to leave quietly, without anyone knowing.* . . .

The next day, I am shipped off like a clandestine package to Addis Ababa.

Book 3

Exodus of Innocence

Outside the fire burned intensely, bursting into gleams of blaze like a flaming desire. Young people obliged the palm of their hands to hover over the conflagration to steal some heat. It was a cold evening in Rome. And the big room that the social center let my friends use to throw a surprise party for our friend Mishael didn't have a heater. So most of us abandoned the music and the dancing inside and sought after heat by the fire outside. Mishael was leaving for a better life (whatever and wherever that was), and it was almost a tradition to throw a party for the leaving ones.

Mishael and I sat on the floor next to the campfire and listened to the sound of the blazes.

Meti, said Mishael, *you got to get the hell out of here. Look at our people. They work at signora houses, cleaning bathrooms and changing diapers for old people. And look at us! We waste best hours and days of our lives at Big, doing nothing but smoke, gamble, and go dancing on the weekend. What kind of life is this for fifteen- and sixteen-year-olds? Our minds are fucked up and can't think any further because all we see is our people bending their back to the lowest places. That's why you gotta get the hell outta here. Here, there's no future for us,* he sadly concluded.

I listened to my friend's words solemnly, gazing into the flames and at intervals turning to look at his face. There was rage in his expression, and when his eyes laid their gaze on the fire, they became one. He burned to escape to a better world. He yearned to be somebody and not just another number in the multitude. And I silently wished him luck with all my heart and forces, for I felt his words and his rage and his burning to be somebody.

The guy who did us the favor of letting us use the place to throw a party, a worker or the head (I didn't know) of the abandoned social center, approached the campfire and revealed to us that there was a story behind those flames.

It's a symbol of memory; something that happened here at the social center several years ago. I will share the story with you later on this evening.

We looked at him without understanding. And I wondered what kind of story would be hiding behind the burning of wood.

Ben, Elkanah, and I left the fireside and the party for a moment to go get candy bars and cigarettes. On our way back, a fashionable young fascist stopped the flow of our walking by standing in front of us. We attempted to move over to the side to get by, but he moved along with us, motioning his body the same direction as us, and prohibited us the right of way. His eyes were filled with contempt, and they looked into ours threateningly. Ben, who was standing between Elkanah and me and had his arms around our shoulders, squeezed us deftly as to encourage us to tolerate this encounter. After the stranger finished insulting us with his gaze and his hands, which floated in his pockets as if to promise the possibility of a weapon, he started throwing words of ice: *You niggers are a fucking curse. You don't belong here or anywhere. Why don't you go back to your fucking country, you fucking shitheads! Negri di merda! Andatevene affanculo! Voi e tutte le vostre razze!*

When he was done yelling, he walked straight through us as if we were invisible ghosts. Tears struggled in my eyes. Ben forced a smile and endeavored to crack a joke but didn't succeed. Elkanah spoke with a heavy knot in her throat, *I lived all my life in this country and never had I anyone insult me like this.* And Meti embittered.

No one was outside by the campfire. Everyone had left the fireside to join the mirth of music inside. The desolate flames looked like a forlorn lover in all her liveliness, yearning to give her unshared passions. Inside, the room busted at the seams and was heated and made lively by the presence of my dancing and rejoicing friends. I went to the front of the room to say hi to the DJ. He came down from the platform to give me the formal *ciao* kiss. There was a mutual liking between us, but I had murdered my feeling for him as for any other guy.

The man who earlier promised us a story behind those flames walked in the room and began his tale.

Several years ago, he said, *an Eritrean teenage boy was burned alive on that same spot where now fire burns. He was from the neighborhood and as you know the kids are predominately fascists around this area and he hanged out with them. But then, he started to come to the social center here and when his friends found out, they were enraged. I guess they felt betrayed. So, one day, the same friends he grew up with beat him to death, dragged his bleeding body right outside this room where all of you were gathered about to get warm. They spilled gasoline on his clothes and burned him alive until only ashes and bones remained. Each time I see that fire, I see his face, his young and full of life face, and despair fills my heart. It's sad to witness what our generation is turning into. . . .*

His voice dissolved into silence in my ears as I turned my attention to my boys and girls who were standing scattered around the room. There was not a girl whose cheeks weren't invaded with poisoned tears. Perez, whom I was told later, was related to the defunct, went hysterical and ran outside and kneeled on the floor by the fire and bawled. And I watched my boys fight back the salty water that swam in their eyes and dangled on their inner lid. Oh, my proud boys! I hungered to know the substance of their thoughts at that moment, for everything about them narrated a tale of tolerance. Tolerance of a lifetime. Oh, my courageous boys! In all your delusion! What would I have given to restore your much-needed pride and self-esteem and hope! I would've renounced my ideals to remove that look from your faces and install some faith in your eyes. That night I thought of a word by which to define my People. Rimbalzanti! Resilient!!!

7

Blossom

Set limits for the people all around the mountain,
and tell them: Take care not to go up the mountain,
or even touch its base. . . .
Only when the ram's horn resounds may they go up to the mountain.

Exodus 18:12–13

THE STATE OF BEING LOST is like walking on a straight line with no curves: You can't make a turn. Or like driving on an unlabeled freeway: You never know where to exit. The state of being lost is being a stranger in a foreign land. It is feeling an outsider in your own skin. Moving to Italy changed my life so drastically that, although I could distinguish the paramount difference between my underdeveloped and shabby-looking native land and Rome's spellbinding architecture, I lacked the skill to understand the shape my life was taking. Part of me was disappointed when I looked at the streets of Rome for the first time. There walked herds of black faces, and I genuinely wondered why in the world everyone portrayed foreign countries so marvelously if their cities didn't exclusively display beautiful white, blond, and blue-eyed people walking on golden-carpeted floors. Piazza Vittorio, an outdoor marketplace, presented a brand-new delusion to my deep-seated illusions. Neapolitan, Roman, Moroccan, and Indian vendors yelled in their customers' eardrums persuasive phrases to sell fruit and vegetables. The same crap as back in Dire Dawa, I thought. The only difference was that, while my hometown was considered poor and worthless, so it didn't matter, Rome was put on a pedestal by millions and there she was slapping me with bitter fingers of reality. Her denizens shouting in my ears words I couldn't comprehend. But balance is the key to everything. A supermarket was enough to open doors to my astonishment. The size of the place and the incredible amount of food and beverages amazed me. Back home, we shopped for our food from the street-dwelling vendors, and the supermarket partly healed my stabbed illusion. And a cross-country trip that made me taste a bite of the voyager Marco Polo's Venezia, Romeo and Juliet's Verona, Pisa's let-me-lean-on-you tower, and Padova, where St. Anthony's tongue was preserved inside a glass case, displayed in the church, completely reanimated me.

Screech, screech, screech . . . It hurts the ear. So many trams and buses and scooters. The sky is blue one minute and gray the next. I keep forgetting this isn't home. How strange it is to watch people act in the bubble of their own little world. They laugh, but I can't make myself follow their rhythm. It goes and travels, reaching places even my imagination can't afford to house. Rome never looked so melancholic, and I never felt this lonely before. I am swallowed by these big-breasted *piazze* and narrow *vie*. I miss home. I miss that dear feeling of belonging. There is no hole deeper than the absence of home. I could scream, using all the chords in my throat, yet no one will hear my voice. It will disappear like a noise of a falling chair. My heart is waiting for a few more invitational knocks to burst out. My fragile heart! Everyone thinks it's unbreakable—*Meti, watch the fire clean down the relics of our damn past. Meti, look how your mother's heart has put out the light.* If only they could see the way their words crash and squeeze and explode and splatter like blood. Maybe it's time to build a wall. A fortress all around. No access. I could let myself float above the ground or sink under the water and not know the difference. Or maybe I should stop hanging out so much with the dead.

I am staying at a charity home. I will name it Mount Sinai. If architecture ever defined anything at all, it defines this abode. The building is built in a classical European style. It is meant to be a moral reform, and one has to besiege the enceinte to flee its threatening rules. The doctrines of the Catholic Church are to be respected to the fullest or one will regret the day she was born. There are four floors. The ground floor displays the statue of the patron saint to greet us. A public and a rotary phone are available for our use between the hours of seven and eight, downstairs. The rotary phone is locked with a key so that we can use it solely to receive calls. Up one flight of stairs, a small church is open throughout the day for the brides of God and for us. On the first floor, there is the refectory for us, the dining room for the nuns, the kitchen, and the playground. Second floor has the privilege of exhibiting the five large rooms for us girls and a privy chamber for the Mother Superior. Each of us is assigned a bunk and a nightstand, but we share the closet. Six or seven girls are roommates in one room. The fourth floor is where the rest of the nuns sleep in their tiny bedrooms with the cross standing on the wall, facing the bed. So here I am, living with nuns and girls from all over the world. Brazil, Cape Verde, Eritrea, Ethiopia, Chad, Italy, Morocco, Portugal, Somalia. We are mixed like a fruit salad, *la macedonia:* watermelon and pineapple and kiwi and mango and papaya and coconut, blending in a bowl of an incorporeal thing called human spirit, sharing a roof and a playground, breaking barriers with language. Did I say language? The other day I learned a new word: *ridere.* I had to say it several times before I could finally explain myself. *Che? Ripetilo un pó! Non ti capisco, spiegati meglio.* My mind racing as fast as it can to catch the new words, register them, make a note. But, for now, let's stick to exploring *ridere. Ridere, no?* I keep saying until I realize that I am placing the accent on the wrong letter. Ah, my darling, my lover, language! How long will it take before I can marry words and play with them, arrange them so well that I could use them to conquer hearts or to hurt them?

Do mirrors talk? Do mirrors slap at insecure girls so hard they turn their faces hot? I watched my face burn this morning as I stood before the looking-glass, my hand holding a toiletry bag, the corner of my eyes stealing moments from the girls who were facing the queue of sinks. Under the surveillance of a nun, we washed our faces, brushed our teeth, and dressed for school and headed downstairs to have breakfast. The murmurs of the mirror still echo in my ears, images that haunt me and grab me by the neck, strangle the sense of certainty out of me. Where do all these enemies come from? How many lives have I lived and how many deaths have I died to gather so much hatred fingering at me? Or am I my own murderer? *Catherine and Heathcliff. Wuthering Heights.*

The pee won't stop. This morning I got up before the sun had risen and before the walking alarm clock came down to wake us up. I took the sheets off the bed, turned the mattress over, and put the blanket on the mattress so that it looked like a made-up bed. Deliberate, Meti, be deliberate. I sat in the hallway, so afraid of what my bladder would do in bed while asleep. I waited for the sun to give a signal that the day was to begin. And I cried. For myself. So much self-pity. Sooner or later this crime of mine will come to light. I will be caught red-handed, holding the wet sheets, and I will be condemned. A sentence that will last a lifetime and harrow me in the form of a bruised pride and a broken heart.

My crime has come to light. Who is this girl wearing a prize-winning cynical expression on her face? Miss Cynical Expression on Her Face. Why is she yelling at me? Who does she pretend to be? *You pee on your bed, huh!!!*

Eeew!!! God, how much I hate girls! They are the worst of people. This moment, this painful instant, this lament in my heart, this weakness in my knees, this trembling of my legs, it could all disappear if I convince the floor to swallow me. Better get on my knees and pray. Pray till I deviate Him from his incessant labor and make some room for me in His busy schedule. *Dear God, if I stop peeing in bed, I promise you, love, I will never again ask you for anything else in this life.* Wish granted. Promise not kept.

Line up in a row. With my best friend Ms Fear. Lice inspection routine. A nun for a judge. She is putting her disposable gloves on, now searching the narrow roads amid our hair for walking, micro-criminals. If any is found, the shelter provider is to wash her hair once and again with a special shampoo that has chemicals that kill lice. If that treatment doesn't work, the nun waves a pair of scissors at the host and shaves her head. I am crossing my fingers. I am shaking. I am praying. *Love, hear my prayer! Did you truly make the lice disappear? Please, don't fail me, not this time. I promise I won't ask you for anything else in this life.* I pass the test. When I tell my sister about my lice-free head, she gives credit to the weather. Only I know the pact between God and me.

We have the privilege of field trips at Mount Sinai. Riding the big Pullmans, the young ones in the front seats, and the older and in-crowd girls in the very back of the bus, discussing knowingly the "Perché lo fai" song by Marco Masini. They swear they know the song is about suicide. *It's so obvious,* they claim. From the front seat, I eavesdrop, dreaming to some day qualify for a seat in the back. I make a note in my head that I have to investigate more this whole affair of suicide. I know it has to do with death. Apparently, somecrazybody grabs a knife, pours a bunch of pills, or ties a rope in a perfect circle and voila, you've got yourself a suicide. I know that much. But what's beyond the idea of performing the act? Why would a teenager slice her precious young veins with a knife? I could ask the girls, and maybe go to the back and mingle with them and throw the question nonchalantly. No. Better cringe in my corner and wait to go back to the city, to the books. Oh, my beloved books! Look what am I reduced to in thy absence!

First stop: the church. Sing in the choir. *Franz Schubert,* "Ave Maria."

Second stop: the plantation. The grape harvest. Pick grapes and jump up and down on the crop.

Up and down Up and down Up and down . . .

I am painting a picture in my head. Watercolor: particles of skin camouflaging in the profuse sweat, materializing in the foul smell that fills the space beyond the canvas.

Meti, you know you don't have to drink it. Stop looking at it as if someone is forcing medicine into your mouth.

Perché non ti fai i cazzi tuoi?

I would mind my own fucking business if you didn't sit here and I would not have to put up with your endless contemplation on the wine as if drinking it were a dilemma of life or death.

A minute ago, the analogy was with medicine and now life and death. Make up your mind.

You're a freak.

Thanks!

She is not the only one who's told me that I am a freak. The boy who likes to repeat every other hour, *I wan thoo go thoo Awaii!* reminds me religiously how much of a freak I am.

Meti, you're so strange. Sei proprio strana, eh.

Grazie!

What else can I do but thank them? However, being called a freak for my revulsion at the idea of drinking the exudation of someone else's sweaty feet is a little uncalled for. So I ask for an explanation in regards to my freak nature.

First of all, you're moody. One minute you're laughing like a mad person and the next minute you're telling us all to go fuck ourselves. Plus, everything has to be questioned. Why can't you just drink the glass of wine? Why do you have to apply a thesis and an antithesis to the bloody drink?

Because your stinking feet were in it.

And yeah, that too. You're fucking rude!

I am sitting on the toilet, reading *Beautiful*, a magazine on soap-opera stars, that confusing day. In Mount Sinai, we're not allowed to read magazines, and bathrooms are our hiding places. Sour Nashson shouts for me to come out, that I'd been in there too long. When I lift my underwear up, I notice a red stain on it. I look closer, and I realize it is blood. Then, when I am about to flush the water, I see that streaks of blood float on the surface of the urine. I flush the water, put my panties on, hide the magazine under my clothes, and leave the bathroom. I don't know what to do or whom to go to. The incident when the girls at the orphanage back home consoled the crying and bleeding girl flashes in my memory. For the first time, I understand the meaning of that episode. I understand, through some kind of an innate sense, that all girls are meant to bleed from down there. But that is as far my explanation can go. I have no clue about what precautions to take, where to go, or whom to go to. Since I am not feeling good, I'd missed school this morning, and I am alone in this enormous place. I go back to the bathroom, roll a good amount of toilet paper, and sandwich it between the inside of my underwear and the open tube that is showering fresh blood. I go back to my room and pace the floor, contemplating what I am to do next. I wallow on the shaky ground of wonderland: Will I bleed forever from now on? Will I have to wear paper forever not to stain my underwear? Will I be the same? I find no answers. I go back to the restroom and look myself in the mirror. And again, I go back to my room and pace the floor back and forth. I am afraid to lie on the bed and stain everything. I go back to the bathroom to check the status of my underwear and the blood faucet. I encounter a blood-soaked roll of paper adhered to the bloody panties. I stand on a lonely floor, gathering courage to confront one of the nuns. Sour Ohad comes up to give me medicine for my headache and when I hear her steps, I run to bed. She scolds me for wandering around. I take the pill and struggle for the words to tell her about my discovery. I can't. I am ashamed to utter such a phrase as there is blood streaming from my vagina. But miracles exist and some kind of force makes me recall a word I heard in that very place, and it is related to bleeding down there: menstruation. I tell her, *Suora, mi sono venuti le menustrazioni.* She smiles a big smile, hugs me, congratulates me, and leaves the room, assuring me she'll be right back. I sit there, wondering why in the world was she so happy for me. I wonder what a strange place the world is. Back in Ethiopia, a young girl bleeds and friends console her as if it is her funeral. Here, a young girl bleeds and the nun congratulates her as if it is her wedding day. Sour Ohad comes back with sanitary pads and new pairs of underwear and sweets. She says this is a big day for me. *Congratulazione!* I fake a series of smiles and leave the room to change into clean underwear, and I am glad to find out about the existence of those magical pads, for it makes more sense than the roll of paper to protect the panties from getting stained. By evening time, the whole world knows about my womanhood. The Mother Superior calls my sister on the phone, and both congratulate me. During dinner, the girls shout to the heavens that I have become a woman. The girls, the nuns, the walls, the skies, all talk. And I hear without listening.

What is it like to be a woman?

Aren't you one already? Plus, what's up with this 'to be a woman' shit! I see no change in me but the fucking blood streaming like dirty water from an old faucet. It's disgusting. It makes no sense.

You should be happy. It's the first step into womanhood.

Womanhood my ass. I could really do God a favor and beat the shit out of Eve if I ever see her during my bleeding phase. This too must be the punishment for her fucking act of eating the apple.

You're a nut case.

I have blood running wild and free between my legs. That's enough to mess with your head. And I want to understand, if you can explain this to me, of course, so while we deal with this shit of putting pads every two hours, getting cramps and moody, what role do men play in this hell of ours?

They work hard.

They work hard? What do they think women do? Sit around and have periods?

That's the ideal.

Well, they don't. And I'm not about to sit around and have periods and exist like a vegetable.

Bearing a numb feeling, I tremble in the unknowns that I see my life is leading me to. I feel lonely, and I gasp for any sigh of presence that will store in me some mettle.

With Zipporah, it's girlfriends at first sight. She is beautiful and quite a threat. And I am jealous, for I know everyone's attention will turn to her and I will be forgotten. And that is exactly what happens. I am no longer a queen even to my own blood. My sister keeps telling me how I should be more like Zippo, who dresses well and carries herself finely and doesn't go around wearing pants all the time like boys the way I do.

Look at Zippo, she'd say, *She's always laughing. Just look at her! She's a happy kid, playful and always with a smile on her face. Oh, Meti, and you need to get rid of that belly of yours. This ain't Ethiopia. Here, slim is beautiful.* And I fume. Then, Zipporah's body and mine develop. Our plain chests blossom a pair of rose buds, our hips broaden like the large leaves of a plant, our thighs and calves become fuller like a trunk to sustain its tree, our behinds stick out like two halves of an apple. We discover boys, but they seem to discover only Zipporah. I exist without being seen. And once again I fume.

Zippo and I escape the sense of imprisonment in Mount Sinai by ditching school. We ride *la metro* to Villa Borghese and lie under a tree and do personality quizzes, waiting for the sun to set and the dusk to fall upon us. We face the sky, exposing the pupil of our eyes to the slanting rays of the sun and exchange our dreams of true love. We sneak in and out of the narrow Roman streets and, when the time comes for our venturing to come to a close, we sit down on the cozy floor and meditate to come up with a plausible excuse to tell the nuns or the family in case they call school and find us missing. But no excuse seems credible enough to miss school and wander the streets of Rome. So we give up and Zipporah says, *Well, our luggage will be waiting for us outside. Hey, at least we have each other.* We laugh, and our temples mate.

The church left behind. I am pure sin. Zippo and I make up our own rules.

THE RIGHTEOUS PATH	THE CROOKED PATH
1. Thou shall not wear miniskirts	1. Take one with you on the way to school and change outside behind a car
2. Thou shall not smoke	2. Unless you're in the premises of the bathrooms in school
3. Thou shall not befriend pornography	3. Do it only when the nuns are asleep

It's thrilling to cheat; to put the thermometer on the heater and fake an outrageously high fever and miss school; to leave the moral reform for school in our decent clothes and transform ourselves into bad girls in a matter of seconds behind a car; to ask permission to use the restroom and use the time to inhale and exhale smoke; to tiptoe downstairs in our socks and watch porn. The pornography sessions in the refectory open to me a world of rapture. I acquire a novel hunger for the experience of the porn stars. I observe how the bodies meet, how the skin becomes the springboard for the lover's submergence. Some day, I too want to come to learn to appreciate the body as something sacred, a treasury storing the highest forms of sensation and ecstasy.

However, one unfortunate evening, an argument begins between Jochebed and Everybody. Jochebed wants to watch the *Witches of Eastwick* with Jack Nicholson and his three women, but the rest of us want to see a South American soap opera. Jochebed argues that it isn't fair, she can't get to watch a movie for once when all everyone sees every *maledetta* week, all

maledetto year, is that *maledetta telenovela.* The nun sides with the major-
ity and says that the *telenovela* is shown once every Monday and if the girls
miss one episode, they'll lose track of the story. Jochebed replies to the nun
that she doesn't care if anybody loses track of it. She is tired of that damn
novela, with the protagonist crying like a baby for two hours, and all that
stupid sentimental language and the disfigured lady hidden upstairs. She
says she has enough of Grecia Colmenares and her misery in love until the
end of the damn *telenovela.* And if for one evening she can't get to watch
her movie, the rest can forget about their *novela* too. Suor Jamin disregards
Jochebed's heated harangue and tunes the TV on *Rete Quattro.* Jochebed
gets up and changes the channel to *Italia Uno.* The nun changes the channel again, using her remote control. Jochebed uses the channel changer on
the TV set. That night the channel changer on the TV set is taped several
times with a very resistant scotch tape. Since the nun keeps the remote
control, we have to wait for Saturdays to satisfy our curiosity about sex. I
join Zipporah in her home, and we stay up late at night and watch those
porno stars share their orgasmic experiences graphically.

When we're not finding smart ways to break the rules and lead an exciting life, we kill time by converting our surrounding into a source of en-
tertainment. Zippo and I sneak in the playground at forbidden morning
hours and play ball. Suor Jachin shouts through the window from upstairs
to stop playing and go up or else. We ignore her and keep playing and
laughing. She comes down and we start to run. The nun chases us in her
habit and after an unsuccessful try to get us she bids us to give her the ball.
The chasing scenario dissolves into the picture of Suor Jachin standing
in the middle, between Zipporah and me, with her hands extended up
high to get the ball that Zipporah and I are passing to each other over her
propelling hands. Eventually, we give in and give up the ball and get
grounded.

In the evening, after we wash up, we go downstairs to watch TV. All
those who speak Amharic, Zipporah, Serah, Korah, Dinah and I, sit in the
back. We gossip about the nuns and whatever forbidden subject we have
in mind. Serah makes the wittiest remarks about everything and cracks
us up and everybody yells at us to shut up. *Vi state zitti!* And if we aren't
laughing at Serah's jokes, we are reprimanding the little girl, who seems to
always shed light on the misery in Ethiopia. Abihu, who is half our age,
likes to bring to everyone's attention how back home people practiced
simple stuff like cleaning their noses. She really tests our patience one
evening when she decides to disclose detailed information to some special

guest the nuns have over. He is unnoticeably using a tissue to clean his nose, and our little friend generously offers to tell him how in Ethiopia we didn't use tissue but the convenience of our hands to get rid of mucus, which eventually wound up on a wall. And she shows him with her hands on her nose, extracting make-believe snot and throwing her hands toward the wall, pretending to stick the aqua-yellow character to it. Of course, everyone is destined to laugh. Everyone but those who know the shameful truth of the narration. We stay quiet, sending a series of threatening looks to the narrator, who subsequently moves her seat as far from us as possible. When the guests leave, we start bombarding with words the little girl who knows too much.

Abihu, my dear, now, did you have to say that? In Amharic.

But it's true. In Italian.

Fucking answer us in Amharic since we're speaking to you in that language. Silence.

Meti, talk to her.

Abi, sweetie, you've to understand that not all of us come from the same place in Ethiopia and not all of us from Ethiopia practice the art of nose cleansing by shooting fireworks of snot against the wall.

Well, I am from Addis and Addis is the coolest city in Ethiopia.

Let me give you access to some information that might be useful to you later on in life. Dire Dawa is the coolest city in Ethiopia, not Addis Ababa. And in Dire, the walls are allergic to snot.

Thanks, Meti! Now, we'll have white people fumbling their way through Addis in their search for an art gallery displaying mucus, said the girls.

The sense of solitude, the chill of fear, and the state of complete loss embrace my being. Breathing becomes as hard as lifting a ton of weight. I cry, but the tears are empty and refuse to lift the load off my heart or the hearts, I wouldn't know. It's a beauty to look in other people's lives and thoughts, yet this beauty is accompanied by pain, excruciating pain of unknown reasons and nondiagnosed diseases and bereavements. I try to focus intently on those lives, squeeze them all into my head. The melancholy. The laughter. The enthusiastic voices. The complaints. The mirth. Make room in my memory. To later remember and cherish forever. But now, now the sadness will go on timelessly. While I watch other people live and respect life, I will find ways to bargain with the past, the present, and the future. I will persuade the vendor named time to have patience with me, to overlook my continuous withdrawal from the race, to forgive my lethargic, unproductive, inconsiderate, and unambitious walk. And this loneliness, this sadness, this sense of fear and complete loss will no longer go on endlessly but will acquire a determinate length. Maybe tomorrow, a very distant tomorrow, I will make the endeavor to be part of the noise, the clatter, the laughter, the silence, the run that goes on outside. Give myself a break from the hell that burns inside. I will finally respect life and won't have to bargain any longer for time.

To save myself from drowning in a flood of tears, I turn to the sea. The sea is like a baptistery. So blue, tranquil, and pure. Zippo and I hitch rides to the beach. We swim to the far-reaching distance of the Mediterranean Sea, take our bathing suits off, and watch the shape our naked bodies in the deep blue sea and feel our skin ferment against the violent waves. We ride the wheel-boats to the same far-reaching distance and dive in the water, naked. We swim further from the boat that is rocking in the middle of the sea, our lonely swimming suits lying on it. Naked is beautiful. The water likes the naked skin and the naked skin likes the water. All loses sense and power when the naked skin and water have intercourse. So I let myself go deeper into the water and further from the sinned-upon earth, closer to the horizon. I watch my body quiver and relax and dance and collide against the violent waves. It is a baptismal experience. The soft caress of the breeze feels like an absolute freedom against my nakedness. The water finds its way in the rift of my genitalia. It fills my inside like semen. I am renewed, possessed, taken to the climax. I am impregnated by the grandeur of nature. My breasts seem to find a niche in the transparence of the fluid. They take the form of two graces taking a bow to the inhabitants of the sea. My hands and my legs are the wings that carry me through this journey. I think how wonderful it would be to be able to use those wings on land, to swim through the tribulations of life, to fight the battles of the heart. For an endless instant, I forget my friend's presence in the water. For an endless instant, I forget the sky over my head. For an endless instant, I forget myself. My solitude, my sense of fear and complete loss have all been apparently abandoned on shore. Left behind. I am no longer a prisoner of cages, cars, doors, ceilings, schools, houses, and buses. I am no longer heedful of streetlights and stop signs. I am no longer a victim or a victimizer. I am no longer the one who breaks delicate hearts or the one that mends them. I am no longer the breeder of blue eras, the captive of yesteryears, the worshipper of tomorrow. I am free. Free in the depth of todays. Free in my nakedness: naked spirit and body. Free. The awe of endless instants is broken by Zippo's violent act of splashing water against my face. We tarry for a while in the nation of purity, swimming, playing with water, and counting to determine the time, which one of us could tolerate to stay under the water the longest. Zippo points out to me how the lifeguards are watching us through their binoculars. But I am not ashamed of my nakedness. Not as long as I stay in the sea. For in the sea, I gain back my innocence. In the sea, Eve hasn't yet eaten the apple. In the sea, I am not part of the crowd of sinning human beings. In the sea, I am born again. At such a young age, life wishes to show me her exquisite corners, the possibilities of joy and peace.

The ascent to the boat, the reunion of the skin with the cloth, and the return to the shore are quite a slap in the face. An awakening that dreamers loathe and would give their reality in order to evade.

For most of my foreign friends, summer was the time when they visited their native lands. I got the unbelievable news that I'd go back to visit Dire Dawa and see all my friends and walk along my former neighborhood's streets. It was a time when I was still in love with my hometown and everything that ever belonged to her. It was a time when the memory tape was erased and innocence and love and beauty so much filled my being that to reminiscence about my childhood years made me the happiest person. Finally, I was to have a vacation, take a break, and for the first time in a long time feel at home. Welcomed. Finally, I was going to say goodbye to all that I'd left behind. But, as John Lennon said, *life is what happens to you while you're busy making other plans.*

Meti, there's no going back to Ethiopia. You just can't go.

They'd have you killed.

Anyway, what would you want to go back there for? Enough of that place!

And we all know this wouldn't be a visit, a vacation.

Dead or alive, they wouldn't let you leave.

I have this outstanding gift to stand still and not utter a word whenever something extraordinarily painful occurs within me. I just listened, nodded something like, *Ow,* and kept up with the sequels to other conversations. Afterward, when I was left alone, I locked myself in the bathroom (bathrooms were always my hiding places) and cried. I looked myself in the mirror and cried. I took a shower and cried. I sat on the bathroom floor, naked, and cried. Then, I lay on my bed and sank into my thoughts. My very incoherent thoughts, whose substance I never seemed to grasp. I recalled one scene, shot many years ago. Mom, the vampire, and I sat on the nasty couch on the veranda and we all laughed and they kissed. Then, I remembered how I've forgotten to return to Shuni the book I had borrowed. I picked up the book and read some passages. How the blonde French lady and the handsome man ran into each other on the street and were each awed by the other. Destiny playing its inevitable role in their lives. How they fell in love. How they parted. Everything passes by; like running water, life flows and slides between our fingers. The curious thing of it all was that I didn't dwell on the reason for my denied return. I just grieved over the disappointment of not seeing all my friends and not walking along those feces-embedded roads and not being able to say goodbye, ever.

8

Initiation Rites

Hunger pushes the hippopotamus out of the water.

Luo proverb

BELA AND I WENT TO THE SAME SCHOOL and developed a bond that no color or race or belief or distance could break. Her magical friendship made me learn the imperative lesson that it was not color or race that stood as frontiers between people. People themselves barricaded the passage into one another's hearts.

It was a special Sunday for my dear friend Bela. Her first communion ceremony, though held at a simple basilica, was to be honored with a visit by Pope John Paul II. Everyone awaited His Holiness's arrival with glee and eagerness. Before entering the church, the first-timers for the taste of Christ's holy body sat in a circle inside a tiny room in the back of the church waiting for God's earthly representative. Even though I wasn't among the celebrating ones, I sat beside Bela amid those white faces dressed in white. I felt like a blotch on a beautiful portrait. Then, the pope arrived in his full grace and made the tour of the small room, giving each creature his blessing. I held tight Bela's hands, for my heart was exploding with an overwhelming emotion. It was Bela's turn. She received the pope's blessing with a smile and a slight bow. Next, His Holiness moved to stand before my undeserving self. He looked at me with an intensity that penetrated my being and asked, *Child, where are you from?*

Di dove sei?

Ethiopia, I answered.

He asked me a couple more questions. His voice smeared my ears like honey, and my heart leaped with joy. He smiled at me, and I returned his gesture. He rested his hands on my guilt-filled head and communicated with his God, brought his fingers down to my undeserving-of-his-touch forehead, uttered his blessing, smiled once again at me, and moved to the side to bless the next person. I sat there speechless. Why did he give more time to the black sheep in the herd of better sheep? Why did he say more words to me than to the rest? Me. A mere blemish.

Adapting to school in an advanced Old World is as difficult as for a wild animal to be tamed. My uncivilized, savage self dives her index finger in the stuffed nostril and digs for archaeological remains before the critical eyes of a classroom's walls. The teacher would walk on me and repeat for the umpteenth time her unoriginal, just-cut-for-my-act phrase: *Remember, this isn't Ethiopia. We don't pick out here. We use tissue.* As soon as I learn the lesson about restraining myself from executing nose picking in public, another problem presents itself. The cultured, condescending girls pick on me constantly, and I lack the constraint or will to hold back from attacking or defending myself with my almost innocent fists. I grab Shaul's long auburn hair as she snaps at my nappy hair until we both fall either on the floor, the desk, or the grand pianoforte. I feel as though I am stepping into a new sphere where I have to be trained all over again how to take baby steps. Nothing makes sense to me. And I make sense to no one. I am only an alien who happens to walk their earthly streets, uninvited, sneaking in their schools, exposing their beauty-accustomed eyes to my unseemly features and incongruous demeanor.

No offense, Meti, but what's wrong with your eyes? You see, one's smaller than the other. It looks dead, Zichri tells me. *And your forehead is so abnormally high,* laughs Zichri.

I swallow the tears, make a deal with rage, and rape will for a smile.

The wild pony is tamed in no time and is able to respond instinctively to the lashes the riders hurl at her. Wild pony loses her freedom and is now a captive. Captive of the formalities, gravities, and exchange traits of this world where acceptance of others costs the priceless price of selling out ourselves.

Professore Hanoch shouts to the class to be quiet, take a seat, and write down the notes on the clef and bass lines. His voice fades into the condensed conversation and guffaw of the class. He sits and stares at one spot, as though oblivious to his surroundings. He has given up on us. I watch him from my front-row seat and feel sympathy for him. I open the notebook with series of five lines and four spaces, and I dot down the lone and legged circles. But the merrymaking in the classroom endears itself to me. The teacher gets up abruptly and tosses his chair heedlessly about the class. The live room is assassinated by the sound of the crash of the four-legged object against the wall. Everyone takes the seat she or he didn't care to take earlier. The teacher returns his *sedia* to its former position and sits on it. He sets his gaze on the same spot as a few minutes ago. I watch him intently: his widely receding hair, the bald spot shining like a glistening mirror; his few-inches-long, thin hair slurring on his neck; his eyes hidden behind the lenses of a pair of eyeglasses. I wonder about that man. I wonder what he feels at being practically ignored by a throng of braying donkeys whose inconsideration reduced him to stare into nothingness. I wonder whether he has a woman at home and if she makes all the cruelties of the day disappear in the magic of passionate kisses and wild sex. I wonder about myself, the inconsiderate self I turned into. I wonder about life. There we were in a beat-up Ethiopia getting blows for not knowing the answer to a question and here I am in a spoiled-child Italy throwing tantrums for being offered the answer to a question. I don't know which of the two is worse.

Professore Hanoch introduces *West Side Story* to his impossible students. We watch the movie and keep Maria company in her sorrow when Tony dies in her arms. After the screening of the movie, the class plagues the halls and the classrooms with the tune and the lyrics from the musical. "America" is the song. Hanoch attempts unsuccessfully to create a choir and to prepare his students for a tentative recital on a short version of the racially oriented, modern Romeo and Juliet. Of course, I am crazy about the song. It narrates the story of my dream. Hanoch says, *Yes, just like that,* and he bids me to stand up and tighten my diaphragm and let my breath reach the higher notes.

> *I like to be in America*
> *Okay by me in America*
> *Everything free in America. . . .*
> *Skyscrapers bloom in America*
> *Cadillacs zoom in America*
> *Life can be bright in America.*

My singing lessons don't last long, and Professor Hanoch fails to bring the play to the stage.

Professore Moses is my favorite teacher, and I am his pet. He teaches Italian and history. It is Professore Moses who sets up my blind date with the concept of heroism. Robin Hood is the first paramour. I read the book, watch the movie, and nothing or no one do I want to be in the world other than someone who is brave enough to stand up for the poor by running over the rich. I resolve to make my duty the dream of dressing in green tights and men's boots and to make history as the first Ethiopian girl Robin Hood. Then, Moses leads our minds to a higher level of thinking by showing us *Schindler's List.* My soul is lacerated. My heart stops. My hands tremble. This time, I lack the imagination to create a Schindler out of me. My hands are just too small, and my soul has not enough incandescence.

Then, the big question shows up at the door. The clueless door of my mind. *To be or not be. Hamlet.* To live life idly while the possibility of greater worlds waits to be chased and grabbed. To perform a variation eternally and to refuse to join the other dancers in the ballet. To move on a single line of thought and opinion when other roads offer the transformation of hearts. To be Meti with no meaningful purpose in life or to be the man who gives up his watch when nothing else is left to relinquish to shed a ray of hope on the fate of an entire race.

So Meti, what's the great plan? asks Professore Moses, concerned about my uncertain future.

They want me to be a nurse.

Who are they?

Does it matter?

You're right. You know why they want you to become a nurse? Because there are plenty of vacancies for that position, right now. "They" want you out and on your own. I agree that you go on your own too because you don't need "them" to put you down, to give you a role unbecoming to your potential.

What do you suggest I do?

I don't have answers for you. What I know is that you have what it takes to do greater things. Don't ever let anyone steal your sense of vision and independent mind.

I replay to Zipporah my conversation with Professore Moses.

Meti, I feel like you're losing your sense of direction. I can't believe you need someone else's reassurance. You should never lose sight of what you have made of yourself. Look at you! Here we are, the bunch of us, lacking no parents, getting free money right and left, trips to Ireland and Greece. But who's standing tall? You. The one without a parent waiting at home with ready dinner, to spoil you with endearing terms and a pile of things that money can buy. You work hard and alone for your place in line. You don't owe to regard anybody in making choices for your future. What happened to "Fuck everybody! I am going to do this and that is all there is to it" attitude?

I'm losing it. It's not easy to pick yourself up after every fall and then to have to stand tall because otherwise they'll see right through your trembling legs and crush you.

The white horse stood on the surface of the swimming pool. The water looked unbelievably calm and the horse had the appearance of a unicorn. For a moment I thought to be hallucinating. But the more I tried to shake the picture out of my sight, the more real the whole thing became. I knew I wasn't imagining it. I knew it was a message from my dad. Perhaps, he sent the horse so that I could ride away from my present life to join him, I thought, recounts our supposed clairvoyant religion teacher to her mind-blown students. She is a blond-haired, average-size, middle-aged woman. Her speech is as charismatic as her persona. I believe her father died when she was young and ever since she has been stalked by these supernatural occurrences. She reveals to us that, although she studied psychology, she always felt clairvoyance to be her best skill.

There were times when I'd wake up in the middle of the night when I was a little girl and find a series of men in their uniforms, sitting up on their horses all over the house, she narrates. *The horse was the key to everything; the answer to the riddle,* continues the clairvoyant woman.

The class listens to her stories, hanging our mouths and our eyes wide open staring at those telltale rosy lips. After class, at lunch, she usually sits at the table that Carmi, Jemuel, Hezron, Pallu, Bela, and I share in the cafeteria. Bela and I often refuse certain foods, stating we are on a diet. She warns us that the first sign of weight loss will show on our breasts. I imagine my to-be-saggy boobs and eat to shake the idea off my head. And I stare at the woman sitting beside me, and I think how she is a riddle herself and I thirst to see beyond.

The deaf-mute students from another class join us during recess, and I watch them silently from my withdrawal. I scratch at their demeanor: the way their hands paint a language with signs and gestures; the way they rest their index fingers in the center of their right cheeks and tilt their hands sideways back and forth, interpreting the good taste of a thing; the way they let their thumbs brush across their cheeks to translate the word *beautiful;* the way they express gaiety by that ringing laughter of theirs. I wonder about their thoughts and their burdens. And I follow with my eyes the steps of a disabled kid's movements, sitting down on the floor, by the wall, left out in the cold yet laughing heartily a laughter that has the sound of dissonant music, free verse. But I am too cowardly to join him or speak to him. And if I do, I shudder with uneasiness for fear of attracting the attention of the edgy-eyed crowd, judging my act of befriending a disabled kid. The revolting cowardice of human nature.

If in Ethiopia my life orbited around the lives of saints and angels and disciples, in Italy celebrities took over from the biblical figures. Television became my best friend and its images my devotion. I became addicted to soap operas and *telenovele*. I mouthed the words to sitcoms and TV series. I replayed video clips in my head. And the turning point of it all was the decision to become a TV star. I was determined to one day be one of those straight-white-teeth smiling faces and unconditionally loving hearts, living a life full of intrigues. I sent pictures to agencies whose addresses I found on the back of teen magazines. But the wake-up call was on its way, ready to loose the sharp teeth of reality on my cheap vanity and misleading illusions. My supposed dream-into-reality-maker agent was up to one thing and one thing only, and that concerned money. First, he shed light on the glamor stardom was to bring. Next, the predator moved to the kernel of the matter and stated that pictures needed to be taken and distributed to various studios and the agency took care of that once I fished 400,000 *lire* from my pocket. Pay in advance. Rise to stardom guaranteed. Take his word. I certainly didn't have that kind of money. So there was my chance of a lifetime blown away. More pictures were sent to different agencies. More interviews took place. More money was demanded of me. I went to audition for a famous TV show called *Non É La Rai*. Wearing a bodysuit and a pair of stockings, I danced to a techno song by the singer of the season, *Corona,* in front of a camera and a jury. They never called me.

Another agency called. The man behind the desk smiled his executive smile and politely offered me a seat. His room was swarmed with pictures of himself with celebrities. I noticed his picture with Ian Ziering, the *90210* star, whom I'd personally met before, and I pointed that out to him. He didn't care to know and instead nonchalantly said, *A great guy.* He explained the contract policy and the purpose of his company. He said that the following Saturday a big audition was going to be held for a group of teenagers, and I surely qualified for that. He explained that the pictures I had sent previously weren't very accurate. They didn't show much and could he see more to be 100 percent sure I met all the qualifications. My fifteen-year-old self said, *Sure.* He had already come around the desk and was standing in front of me. He politely asked me to stand up and unbutton my vest.

Perché?

I just told you. I want to make sure your figure meets all the qualifications.

I unbuttoned the beige vest I was wearing and asked, *Can I not take it off?*

Naturalmente.

He stood staring at my bare belly and white-laced bra covering my pear-shaped breasts.

He said, smiling, *We gained a little weight, eh? It doesn't matter. You just need to watch your diet for the next few days and you'll look perfect. Let me see your hips,* he asked with a professional tone.

I unbuttoned my jeans and showed him the front of my black underwear along with my hips, thus displaying the full length of my seminaked upper body. His eyes fixed their gaze on my bare brown skin.

Beautiful. Why don't you take the pants off? Just to make sure, he said endearingly.

Some kind of providence provided me with a little sense in my naïve head, and I buttoned my pants and my vest and said, *I don't think that's necessary.* He lifted his hand as though he was a criminal throwing the towel in after a long chase by the police. He gesticulated and said, *I just wanted to help you; give you a foretaste before the big day. Just make sure you'll be here at this and that hour next week, with an adult since you're a minor. Good luck! I will see you then.* I left his office disconcerted, unconsciously making the decision that I'd never go back to that office or to any audition or anything else that had something to do with anything where one had to humiliate oneself that way.

9

Colorfield

Characteristic of abstract painting in which large, flat areas of color are spread to cover the entire canvas and dominate over form and texture
Webster's Unabridged Dictionary

PEOPLE OF THE UNIVERSE have proudly divided into groups and each group has constructed a zone, fortified with walls so high and edges so sharp that they scare away and prohibit the right of way to anyone who does not belong to that specific group. To become a member, one has to have the same color, same race, same heritage, and a lot of pride in one's roots. I find making segregation a fashion almost as wrong as imposing it.

The Ethiopian community organized a month-long trip every summer. I participated one summer. A group of girls and boys along with some staff members ventured off on a trip that was going to be quite an adventure.

We sojourned in a small town in the province of Latina. The girls and the boys were separated into two different large rooms with several bunks and night stands. But sleep was the only thing that took us apart, for we were at all times in each other's rooms. We were free like hippies. We went about the house seminaked. The boys were topless and the girls wore barely anything. We smoked after a meal without the need to hide. We played cards and punished the loser with tolerance-testing trials like drinking several bottles of water or taking a shower with clothes on or taking off our clothes. When we were bored, the boldest ones gave the rest a striptease while everybody hummed the *9½ Weeks* movie theme song.

We commuted to the beach every day. The beach at night was my favorite place. I took my shoes off, threw whatever I was holding onto the rocks, and jumped in the sea with my clothes on. My friends yelled at me not to.

Meti, what the fuck are you doing? You can't go in there with your clothes on! Are you crazy? That water must be freezing! It's in the middle of the night. You know the kind of fishes that may be wandering in there, they shouted.

I swam and swam until my feet could not feel the floor any longer. I turned around and, stirring my legs to be able to stand in the water, I invited my friends over.

Come on, ragá, I shouted. *It's the most amazing feeling. É stupendo. Semplicemete divino.*

My words must have convinced them, for I saw them one by one entering the private part of our world, the sea. We splashed the water at one another. We swam and regretted leaving our newly acquired freedom in a place that wasn't polluted with human sin.

Completely wet and barefoot, holding our shoes in our hands, we went up on the street where vendors tried their luck under the night light. We fed our curiosity with the exploration of unusual objects. My eyes landed on a very interesting and, for me, new word. It was the title of a book. I picked the book up, and I looked at the word closer, just in case my probing it attentively might give away its meaning, but it didn't happen.

Hey, ragá, what does Kamasutra mean?

They ignored me. I put the book down. I went closer to my friends, who were walking away from me, and I yelled after them.

Ao, I'm talking to you. Che vuol dire Kamasutra?

All of them whispered, *Shhhh!* tilting their heads and looking at me stealthily and reproachfully.

Don't fucking tell me to be quiet. I just wanna know what the word means. Why are you making such a big deal? If you know the meaning, just tell me what Kamasutra. . . . I was interrupted by Tola, who walked backward, seized me by my elbow, and whispered in my ears, *It's a sexual position. Now, shut the fuck up! You're embarrassing us.*

It was late into the night and we were getting ready to go to bed when Dinah accidentally hit her head against the bed rail. Blood oozed from the wound. I took my undershirt from my bed and taped the open wound with it. Someone brought a wet towel, and I wiped the blood off her face. They got a car and took her to the hospital. She got stitches and was in pain for several days. She couldn't chew, so whatever she put in her mouth had to be liquid. But one evening, we were having a pie, and she told me how much she was craving for it, and could I help her eat it. Could I please chew it for her? I shook my head with disgust.

Eeh Dinah, che schifo! I'm not gonna do that. That's disgusting.

Dinah insisted, *Meti, please, I'm the one who's gonna eat it. E dai?*

I surrendered and chewed the crust and, twitching my face, put it on my hand and passed it over to her mouth. She swallowed the pie and beseeched me for more. I chewed for her a couple more bites, but I couldn't stand to see her swallow what had been in my mouth and left her side, ignoring her imploring words.

The boys all stood around my bed, with their hands stretched wide out, their eyes lifted up to the ceiling, standing in a trance. Aaron wore my blue sheets around him, rendering my bed naked, and led the ceremony. Gershon repeated this after him. When I walked in the room, they all started uttering fake sobs and swarmed around me with condolences and pats on my shoulder. Aaron and Gershon held my idol's poster and announced, *Meti, we have unfortunate news to give you. Mark has left us this morning. He is no longer sharing this world with us. I am so sorry.* And Gershon gave hysterically comical sobs. Mark was a member of an English band whom I was crazy about, and that scene was supposed to be a funeral to mark his fictitious death that my friends had put together to scare me and entertain themselves.

How dare they talk to us like that! How dare they! Even those fascists that live in my building never called me names. The worse is that these bourgeois men sit around, wearing their nice clothes and fake smiles, playing the role of respectable men. At least those fascists cry out loud where they stand. And the mayor! God, he just sat there without uttering a word when the whole town was insulting us like that. And to think that just last week he was talking about having Dinah and Meti compete for Miss Italy. He's full of shit. That's what he is. Fake hypocrites! I hate this town. I wanna go back to Rome, shouted Aaron, his voice raging with anger.

We were all gathered in the boys' room. I stood in the doorway and was stricken by the grave expression evident in everyone's face. The town's old men had told some of the boys, the ones with the wrong color, to get the fuck out of that town. And of course the boys had to wait until they were safe where no one could hear them to protest against the injustice. You know, when you fall down and hurt yourself and a swollen bump grows on your knee and you shake with pain? That was how I felt. A hard lump grew within me, and I had to hold myself to restrain tears from exiting. I shook so hard I had to walk away to kill the pain I was feeling at hearing those words and looking at those grave faces. The mirror was a cruel friend.

Sour Nadab is the cook at Mount Sinai and has the power on all the kitchen-related issues. She is from the south of Italy, and her accent is so heavy that her voice rings like a distinct church bell, a knell, when she shoos us away from the kitchen. I am mopping the floor in a hurry because

I am running late to school. Sour Nadab shouts at me to do my job properly and not leave the pavement looking like a muddy road. I tell her that I have to rush because I am going to be late to school.

Scuola, mi nonna! School, school! Stop that nonsense and clean up! Sgoba, sgoba that'll be more useful to you. You're gonna end up being a maid anyway. When have you ever heard of a negra in school!

Her speech keeps me company until I finish mopping. Everybody else always laughs at the things that she says, for they find her bold manner and speech funny. I don't know what to think of her, and she certainly doesn't strike me as a funny person. Instead of making me laugh or upset, her words disorient me.

It is a holiday. Christmas perhaps. The buses are not running, thus nowhere but the walking distance in the neighborhood could be put on our list of places to go to. Both Zipporah and I are in good spirits, for the day happens to be one of those days one feels manic. Zipporah suggests we go to Piazza Dei Mirti, and, if we are lucky, we'll find an open bar. We do. We eat some pastries. Then, the two girls go a-wandering, walking aimlessly, laughing at each other's jokes, listening to each other's stories. A car comes speeding and I almost go under it, but my friend pulls me back, avoiding the fatal crash. A block ahead, a dog barks heatedly and jerks violently as he sees us approaching. I get scared and take a step back.

The owner, an old lady, says, *Don't be afraid! He does that every time he sees colored people. He just barks and barks at them.*

And the dog barks and barks at us as he passes my very scared and Zipporah's laughing self. She keeps laughing, and I ask her what is it that she finds so amusing.

She says, *Did you hear what the lady said? Meti, even dogs don't like us. Even dogs don't like black people. Ha, ha, ha, ha, ha. . . .*

I look at my friend with a face as grave as darkness and say, *Vaffanculo, Zi! This ain't funny.* Deep inside, I truly wish I were like my friend. I wish I too could laugh at being demeaned. Oh, how I wish heavy thoughts didn't race so restlessly in my head and hot tears didn't dangle so close to my eyes.

It is a beautiful day, and I am on my way to the nearest bookstore to buy a diary. A strange-looking man comes out of the blue and bombards me with icy words, right upon my aloof hearing, lately wont to listen to the sound of silence. I turn to look, thus give a face to the shouting voice, and see the madman start racing after me. Disconcerted, I too run for fear he might catch me and finish with this idle life of mine. He calls after me, *Negra! Merda! Get the fuck out of here! Go back to your fucking country! Maledetta negra!* And he runs and screams and runs after the one he thinks is a curse to his nation or, to use the word he uses, *una maledizione* [*a malediction*] *to his country and his race.* And I run, my heart in my mouth, beating like outrageously fast-paced music. My eyes shed hot tears. My legs shake like a tree trunk during an earthquake. And I run and regret being born and wish I had deteriorated in the squalid reality of poverty I was born in. I run and wish I didn't have to wear the skin I am wearing and I wish I didn't have to live my entire life being a beggar for acceptance, a mere intruder, a foreigner, an immigrant, an expatriate, a fugitive in other people's country. I run and wish that the violent blows of the wind would take me away with the rest of the dead leaves. I run and wish that the ruthless floods that so often visited my hometown had taken me away with the rest of the underprivileged children and beggars of this cruel and unfair world.

My friendship with Bezalel had sown its seed one summer in the parks of Rome where the two of us went to jog and lose weight but instead we lay on the grass and gained conversations. She reserved a table at a restaurant somewhere in Anagnina to celebrate her seventeenth birthday. When a group of us arrive at the place, the restaurant is half-packed, and our table stands out like an empty, white wall in a lively decorated room. We sit, and no server seems to notice us for a very long time. Bezalel goes to remind the manager of her reservation and let him know that we are there. After several tries of eye-hunting and hand-waving to get the attention of a server, finally one of them comes to our table and is nice enough to tell us there will be a wait. And we wait. We wait for more than an hour, and no sign of people approach our table to let us know anything or offer us some water. We all start to get upset along with our stomachs.

Naphtali says, *This is the treatment we get for being black.*

Bezalel gets up and goes to ask whether we're ever getting food. They tell her we will. The guests who occupied the many tables when we got there have eaten and left. New parties take their place around a table and are served by very obsequious servers. We watch them enjoy their food, push their empty plates over for the server to take away, and smoke their after-meal cigarettes.

Naphtali says, *That's it! I'm leaving. For God's sake, we've been waiting literally for hours. The people who came here after us have been served and left and not one time we were approached with a word of courtesy. We had to go and inquire. And for what? To be told to wait and consequently be ignored. I know racism is part of reality but, damn it, Bezalel's father reserved in advance for this dinner. And it's obvious they're ignoring us on purpose. I'm leaving.*

Naphtali gets up to leave, but the boys tell him to sit down and shut the fuck up. Bezalel goes once again to speak with the people in charge of the restaurant. Eleazar tells Naphtali, *You're a prick, Naphtali. Why don't you have some respect for Bezalel? It's her birthday. Do you have to ruin it by saying how unfair this and that is, and worse yet by leaving! You think we enjoy waiting for hours like this? But it ain't Bezalel's fault if these people are racist. That's life.*

Naphtali replies, *Fuck, that's life. I'm leaving.* And he walks out.

Benjamin says, *Ragá, Naphtali is right. I mean we've been waiting here for like three hours.*

Bezalel comes back wearing a gloomy face and sits down silently. The boys go outside to get Naphtali. After we witness the exodus of the throng and the dwindling of the objects and leftovers on the tables, someone eventually resolves to waste some time on the left-out-in-the-cold table, which now shines like a naked body on a plain canvas. When we are finished eating and leave the restaurant, it is past midnight. The buses have stopped running. We resolve to walk to the nearest terminal, where we can find a few nocturnal buses in service. Since we aren't very familiar with the area, we consider taking the bus route. But Benjamin suggests we take a shortcut under his guidance. We get lost and wind up walking for hours, strolling along the long sidewalk, our profile facing Cinecittà, the world of movies. Eleazar and I walk next to each other, heading the march of a group of teenagers whose lives have just been scarred by another bitter episode to be added to the cicatrices of the past and the many others to come.

The bus seems to be exploding with beauty. I stand in the back and breathe in my friends' happy faces and voices. Moments like these are my favorite. I want to stop time. Stay forever on the bus, with my rejoicing friends and with my crowded heart. I don't know whether it is the magic of the ringing laughter or the strange motion of the vehicle, but something about this moment captivates my being and makes me happy to be alive. We are on our way to Mishael's farewell surprise party.

Who will be my lucky coin, now? Mishael had asked me earlier this afternoon at Big.

I thought the purpose of your departure was to get away from this life, I said. The night before he had used my hands to hold the cards he'd gambled with and had given me the credits for his victory.

Our stop approaches, and I dread to leave my crowded heart on the bus. A large cold room, a campfire, hip-hop music, pleasantries, embraces, deep talks, tears, and a tale of murder are written in the stars for us tonight.

You're OK?

This is a typical start to the stimulating conversations between Bezalel and me.

I am great. You?

Yeah. You know, we never take things as intensely as you do. We're no poets.

I'm no poet, either. And you don't have to be a poet to be broken by the story we've heard last night.

The story we heard last night had to do with the boy who was burned alive.

That's the destiny of immigrants.

To be burned alive?

To be burned one way or the other. We are the tale of sacrifices.

Sometimes we've no choice.

Of course we do. We didn't have a choice back home when we knew by heart the language of a hungry stomach and when people had to pass impossible exams to get into universities that fitted fucking two people. Then, we didn't have a choice. But, here, we're pulling the trigger with our own hands. Nobody is going to make me feel bad for being born black and poor. I've the right to be here and to be happy like anybody else. And if someone thinks that 'cuz his shoe shines from the outside and conceit lies under his nose he's better than me, fuck him! No idiot is going to convince me that I'm worthless just because he had all his life those things that I was denied. Outside we're nothing but pretty people and mannequins for the display of aesthetics. What am I to do with that? Place it on my vanity and stare at it? There's so much to a person, and if people are not able to recognize what lies beyond the appearance, then, that's their problem. I am going to get the shiny shoe and indulge myself, I'll admit that. But I wanna make sure that I'll nurture the foundational rock that carries me from the inside.

You're too idealistic. I think that's going to bring you lots of disappointment in life and many many sessions of pipponi mentali. And those are never fun.

Of course, they are. You make lots of immaculate babies called values.

It is Bezalel who introduced the term *pipponi mentali* to me. Mental masturbation.

He introduced himself as a fascist. He showed me the German flag attached to his jacket sleeve like a tattoo. He said I should know that *der Fuhrer* and *il Duce* were made out of the same cloth. Both fought in the Great War, both suffered terrible deaths, the former suicide, the latter lynching, and both went down with their women, Eva Braun and Clara Petacci. He was going to name his daughter Clara when he had one. Did I know anything about the Third Reich? That Hitler was something. Did I know he wanted to be an artist? Thank God he never became one! Waste such a mind in drawings and paintings. *Roba da terzo mondo!* No offense. The third world had its charms, too. Me, for example.

Ao, what are you doing?

I'm talking to Meti. Have you two met?

She's black!

She's the coolest black I've ever met.

You don't know any blacks.

Well, then, she's the only cool black I know in Rome.

He wanted to know about Ethiopia. Was it a jungle down there? He'd always had fantasies about jungles. Living among cement all his life. Old motherfucking cement! Did I ever go to the Colosseum? That place was falling apart. Someone needed to tell those people that change was necessary. That was what the Blackshirts were about. Change. All this sentimentalism for old buildings and history was bullshit. Radical change was the secret to leading a country. Mussolini did his best, but he was a copycat. Hitler was the true radical. Oh, shit, he was running late to the demonstration. It was fucking cool to talk to me. Ciao! That was when the fascist kissed me on the cheek and left.

You see what you do for not taking a stand in a political movement, Meti. You attract everybody. Even parasites named fascists. Nooo good, Meti! said the communist.

She was writing on students' diaries quotes by Mao-Tse Tung. Another girl came holding high a thick book and hit it hard against a desk. It was the biography of Ernesto "Che" Guevara. She said she was going to be the best communist ever. No more amateur business of wearing those black and white Arab scarves around her neck and red t-shirts with Che's portrait in black and marching down the streets of Rome holding pickets that read "Bread Not War." It was time to get serious. She was going to read everything Che, Mao, Marx, Lenin, and Castro had ever written. Stalin? Stalin was a shame to the Society of People's Commissars. How were the gulags different from the Holocaust? He was never meant to lead the Bolshevik Party in the first place. Lenin had chosen Trotsky to take his place. Did I know Stalin meant man of steel? Man of steel her ass! He was a thief. What did she expect from a man who was trained to be a priest? I should know that God had no role in communism. The Church be excommunicating people all the time, well, guess what, the communists excommunicated God. That was what she called revolution! So much to learn. She shouldn't ignore the poets, either. Neruda. And the philosophers. Camus and Sartre. It was important to stay in the circle, though. It was like those Christian fanatics who didn't want you to read anything except the Bible. No need to be influenced by outside voices. And her bible will be the canon by communist writers.

Hip-hop is not just a type of music. Hip-hop is a philosophy.

And he was a black soul trapped inside a white body. But what did I know! Me and my white music. I had no business listening to pop and rock crap. Take That? What was wrong with me? Never forget my roots. Rap and hip-hop, baby!

I'm tellin' ya, those hunter-gatherers be shakin' that ass to Salt 'n' Pepa's "Shooperu," and rapping about bitches and Mercedes-Benz.

Always with my sarcasm. We couldn't afford sarcasm in this white man's world. We had to eliminate racism off the map. One Power! His friend, a black soul freed inside a black body, joined us holding a book. Malcolm X by Alex Haley and Malcolm X.

I always found reading to be a chore, but this is the good stuff.

He had a dream now. He wanted to do time in prison so that he would have a chance to come out enlightened. Prisons had divine lights. We spent too much time dancing hip-hop, listening to Snoop Dogg, singing "No Woman No Cry," when instead we should have been fighting. That black man from America knew exactly what we needed. We needed to kick ass. Nothing could come out of nonviolence. Did we know that Malcolm used to be a hoodlum? Just like us. Look at us! We were a bunch of losers. Drinking. Smoking. Gambling. Clubbing. Hooking up. Stealing. If we were this lost at fifteen, sixteen, where were we going to be at twenty-five, twenty-six? In Palermo as the African Mafia from Big? It was time to get Muslim. Orthodox was not for us. Islam was the religion for blacks. Christianity was imported to Africa by the white man.

Islam was in Africa waiting for the Arabs to emigrate. I remember.

Always with my sarcasm. Did I expect him to jump up and down around a fire like a madman, worshipping weird spirits and sacrificing people and cutting his face and shit? That was not a religion. That was some spooky shit. Islam was what transformed that X man overnight. He was a hoodlum one day, and the next day he woke up Muslim and a revolutionary. That was it. He'd done the hood thing. All he had left was prison and a change of religion.

10

Novillada

(Bullfight with young bulls
and novice bullfighters)

IS THE HEART REALLY A HOLLOW ORGAN pumping the blood it receives from the veins into the arteries and not a deep well full of riches pirates of the sea and thieves of the land have been hunting ever since time began? Here goes my story. I carried a jar with me the last two times I went to see him. A jar so wide and tall that every few minutes I had to stop and rest from walking. In the meanwhile, I made a list in my head. The things to carry back with me. In the jar. His cologne-ridden smell. The stain of sweat on his undershirt. A flash of his smile. And his eyes. Please, let me not forget his eyes! One sound of his rage and another from his silence. Instances of his touch. Lost in my thoughts, I stumbled and tripped over my jar twice.

He received me with a complete indifference. Not an ounce of love in his voice. Not an ounce of hate in his eyes. Those eyes. Let me start my packing with the eyes. Intense like the night. Shaped like a cat's. Then, I noticed the stain on the collar of his shirt and smelled his sweat. I have to come back for his cologne-ridden scent, I thought, and also for the one sound of his rage and for the instances of his touch and the flash of his smile. I returned home with my jar half-empty. His eyes and his silences pulled at my sleeves importunately in their demand for my undivided attention.

At home I sat on the floor and unpacked the jar. I smelled his sweat. I listened to his silence. I gulped down his eyes. The tears came down my face like the foams of the waves washing the sand ashore. Liking him hurt. I liked him until I got weak in the knees and my stomach went hungry. I liked him for reasons unknown to me. He was the one to decide (nonverbally) that the fire couldn't be kindled between us. That the kisses he had given me had taken the form of ashes. I failed to see the ashes, and his demeanor accused me of denial. His demeanor insisted that I had been mistaking for fire the flower that he planted on my lips as a present on my birthday and on New Year's and I refused to throw away when it grew dead. It's a dead flower you see for Chrissake. *La fleur que tu m'avais jetée dans ma prison m'était restée; flétrie et sèche, cette fleur gardait toujours sa douce odeur! Carmen. Bizet. The gypsy and the soldier. Why can't he obsess about me like Don José? Why can't I be free like Carmen?* But I was a prisoner of his image and his indifference. Wake up! Dead flower. Not fire. Dead flower. Not fire.

Well, fire still burned in me. Of anger. Of misery. Of regrets. But mostly of tenderness. He was the first boy I ever liked. The horse on the pedestal. The heroic warrior. The protagonist of every movie. The title of those Victorian novels. A younger version of Mr. Rochester. And the teacher. The lesson of obsession consists mainly of acquiring a taste for touch. Everything transcends from the touch. It was his touch that taught my head to swerve and my emotions to dance wildly. It was his touch that taught my lips to grow ablaze and my hands to desire. It was his touch that introduced nostalgia to my flesh. His touch. So I longed for him, lying alone on a cold floor, tracing in my mind the places that he had traveled on my skin. More tears fell. More knots formed in my throat. More images ran in my head. He and the substitute tree. What is this need for one thing to be discarded so that another could start? I put his belongings back into the jar and walked back to Big to see him. He was neither surprised nor pleased to find my inadvertent presence before him. His persistent indifference felt like a tightening rope around my neck. This time, I was able to steal his cologne-ridden smell, one sound of his rage, and a flash of his smile. That night, I left with treasures lavishing in the jar. I guarded the gems in the vault of my mind until they started disappearing gradually, one by one. What I had left was an empty jar and the embers of memory.

He came like a sequence of waves in my life. Although I could see it arriving, the impact of every emotion was sudden. Each one engulfed me entirely into the deep and unknown sea. It was almost impossible to reach the surface of the water, let alone the shore. You know when those toothpaste TV commercials show the image of someone smiling and the model has that diamond-like tooth standing out and making the click sound. That's exactly the effect he had on me the first time I saw him. Though with him, not just the tooth, but everything else stood out. The a cappella of his smile, the tempo of his talk, the cadence of his voice, the ballad of his ways, they all harmonized with one single click sound. I was barely a teenager and although I didn't know it then, meeting him was the entrance to a door I would later seek for years so that I could find my way out.

A lightening has broken in the window of this walled heart. Oh, how bright and striking is its light. I never knew the presence of a person could place the sun in such a dark site. I should grasp as many rays as my thoughts can house and hold them captive here and study how they move and breath and dance, dance wildly, round and round, and crush against me. He is dancing with me. He is killing me with the scent of his perfume, which is adhering to my memory to later haunt me every second of the minute. I lose my breath. Can the touch of a boy reduce a girl to pure obsession? I can't stop thinking about his hands traveling around my clothed body. His hands. I never knew hands could speak, have a language of their own. I am trying now to remember their words, decipher their meaning. Will I have to learn another language to understand his hands? His hands. They grip my waist as if I were delicate porcelain. They walk up and down my back like the caress of the wind. Is he the wind? Appearing from nowhere in my life, slapping my standing existence with his violent motions, speaking the language of hands. He must be the wind, a messenger from distant lands. The song is over. Everyone is leaving the dance floor. Everyone but us. Those hands are now around my head and his lips are on mine and I am lost. Where am I? What is this? Who is he? A shiver takes hold of my body. My heart is pounding, growing longer legs perhaps. I am turning away from him, but he won't let me. He grabs my wrist and draws me closer to him and asks me whether I am ashamed, embarrassed. I can't answer him that. I don't know how or what I am. I am lost, disoriented. What does the encounter of a boy's and a girl's lips represent? What is this feeling that's parching down my throat, boiling like hot water for chocolate in my chest? Hot water for chocolate. My girls, who apparently witnessed the scene between the wind and me, are congratulating me. Shall I ask them to define this whole thing for me? Perhaps, they speak the language of hands. How ignorant of me to have lived fifteen years in this life and still not know the language of hands!

Days are walking by like a tortoise. The two desperate hands of the clock seem paralyzed. I want to see him. I create the scenario in my head, but the imagination fails to do justice to his beautiful self. I must see him in person. New Year's is the occasion.

One of the boys attracts everyone's attention by announcing the news about a couple having sex inside a car. We all head to the car. The object of my obsession is walking beside me. He puts his arm around my shoulder.

Are you cold?

Yes.

He extends the arm that's around my shoulder to reach my hands, and he holds them with his. I feel the warmth of his body and the breeze of his breath and the coolness of his cheek. We reach the car, but no one, not even the promise of two bodies in motion, is inside or anywhere near it. Everyone curses at the one who brought us all to witness what we didn't.

Ma vaffanculo! they shout.

I swear they were in here a moment ago.

They leave one by one, leaving trails of disappointment along the way. Why were we all so eager to see two people perform the act of sex, I wonder. The inexperience of youth.

My aunt's car is down there. Why don't we go there and talk? suggests Mishael.

No! we reply, Zippo and I.

I turn around and realize that everyone but the four of us were left there. The object of my obsession and Mishael insist we go to the car.

With the condition that we talk like friends, nothing more, I say.

I know my statement is an undercover agent for my feeling for the wind, a sentence made out of cheap words and even a cheaper meaning. But I don't care for meaning right now. I just want to drink in the unrepeatable moments, the fleeting instances, and the unspeakable, indescribable things of life. We walk to the car. Zippo and Mishael get in the backseat. The wind and I take the front seats. He talks, but I don't understand his words. I am too busy gulping down the moment. I am feeling drunk on his presence, his smell, his voice, his touch. His presence that tastes like cheesecake but feels like tequila once the alcohol is inside the body and drives it reckless. I look for balance and talk. Talk nonsense. *Che vuoi dire con questo no come comunque avevi detto facevi bugiardo non é vero . . .* Crush!!! He stops the train of my speech and thought with his lips. He drives them straight against mine. He delves his tongue into my mouth like a car into a tunnel. I had only a vague idea that the tongue is part of the kissing process. Since the first time he kissed me he'd stopped at my lips; his tongue caught me by surprise now. What is this mating of tongues, this brushing of bodies, this encounter of the skin? He feels like the breeze of the wind on my skin, like spring, like May. He is air and colors and trees and flowers. He tastes like chocolate in my mouth. His whole being, his movements, his smell, his touch, his story, his poetry, his desire, his sins melt in my breath. His lips and tongue vibrate mine, making my emotions play like a unison of string and wooden instruments. He leads me out of the car. We walk. His impatient steps throbbing like an anxious heart beside my fearful and reluctant crawl. His hands caress the skin that is adhered to my slender neck the way mild water flows on a naked flesh, tickling. No one has ever been so close, so intimate to me before. We stand against a car and kiss under the starry sky, the night folding us with her magical atmosphere. I feel my body go on fire and imagine the flames burning down the cars and buildings around us. He is kissing my neck and back to my lips and I am living his transformation from a human being to a burning wood. Burn for me, darling, burn for me! I can't breathe. I can't move. I can't speak. He shoves his hands under my sweater and slides them up my belly to halt at my breasts. He inspects the laces of my brassiere, touching them first softly, then with a fervent movement of his hands. I can sense his erect penis behind his clothes as he lifts his body up and then brings it down. Up and down like an elevator. I am losing myself. I can't feel my arm or lips: both seem entangled in his. He is burning me with his burning, reducing me to ashes. Perhaps for his convenience perhaps for my own ashes I can be and he an urn and I could settle in him eternally. Belong to someone finally. But before things get out of hand and this kissing without commercials leads to something more involved, I say to my urn that we should go back to the party and mingle with the crowd. Holding hands, we walk back to the hotel and join our friends in their dancing to Eritrean jams.

I am surprised at finding myself not ashamed of the night of passion-ridden kisses and caresses. My memory rejoices at the sensation the remembrance of his touch evokes. Mom, the church, God, the past are actually abandoning my person in layers. I don't endeavor to struggle against the pleasure or attempt to stifle the experience of my flesh. The guilt the personages of the past had obliged me to feel seems to lose its domineering power over me. I lie on my bed and brood over thoughts I never imagined I could raise. I retrace with my fingers the places where his hands have visited. I daydream of him, of scenes never acted by the two of us as our entangled bodies rolled on the beach. I fantasize of dialogues and soliloquies of love declarations never performed by the two of us, and I smile at the thought of those words and the beauty that emanates from them. My heart is ready to be trampled upon, dilated by the entrance of an outsider, quaked by new emotions, leveled to the heights of risks and the depths of possibilities. I know this heart of mine is as raw as my age. Yet, I have accessed the world of emotions. However limited is my view and however disadvantaged are my legs from entering the door completely, I am still thrilled to take a peek.

He ever sways and dances in my eyes. His presence brings joy, offers love, and gives life. It's not butterflies that he evokes to scatter in my chest. It's blood that he evokes to swerve—hot blood that reveals the existence of life. I feel like I'm dying and then living again. And I am dancing, once again a child, once again alive. You give me life, darling, deliver me from this darkness. Own me. Inhale me as if I were windy air, and convert me into a worshipper of your hands and face and words. I could hang to your words and dress them and make them so pretty you won't recognize them because they will become mine. Mine. My religion will you be. I promise my lips will adore you. They will discern the surface of your movements; extract the opal of your thoughts. I will frame your glances in my head and nail them to my heart. I will save your kisses and wear them like tattoos. You will be my direction and civilization and inspiration and strength and beauty and courage and reason to laugh or cry and believe.

He won't see me the same way I see him. He won't cherish the moments spent together the way I do. My heads is swirling and racing back and forth, turning over ideas, grilling what-ifs. What if I tell him how I feel and he doesn't reciprocate? What if the vulnerable words of love are ridiculed and derided by his nonchalance? What if my pregnant eyes encounter his indifference? I've to defy what-ifs and act. I declare my feelings through a poetic letter. Well, there comes his presence in shape of uncomfortable silences and glances. Now, what to do with myself? Cry, stay in bed for weeks, and lament over my unrequited obsession. I want to grow empty. I don't ever want to experience this thrust of swords inside me.

It burns. I am reduced to a piece of paper that burns under the sight of his hands circling her shoulders. He pours his kisses like God's hands pour rain on earth. He chose her to be his earth, not me. Oh, it burns! I hold my tears back and face him and her. I make an effort, an excruciating effort to embrace that image: the one who resuscitated my heart from old graves and the other who's placed in his heart. Things happen for a reason. God knows why he does things. No one can take away what's yours. It's not meant to be mine. Not meant to be. Can't fight the tears anymore. I've got to run. Run far. The bathroom. My hiding place. The mirror talks to me. You shall never be vulnerable. Never be fragile. Never. How can you give heart legs and set it free on such an adventurous voyage? Wipe your tears. Hold your head up and take back what you let out.

Time intensifies my desire for him. I want him. I want him badly. He's become food for my thoughts, words for my poetry, and a prayer for my conversations with God. Everyday, I starve for his touch and his voice and the look on his face. My lips crave for his, and they grow sore and dry like a dead tree in winter. I hunger for his hands to bring warmth, for his eyes to own me. I pick up the phone and dial his number. I can't bring myself to speak. *Pronto! Pronto! Chi parla?* His voice spreads like jelly in my ears. My hands shake. My legs grow weak. I hang up.

It hurts. It hurts to see him. It hurts to hear his voice. It hurts to smell him. It hurts to like him, to think of him, think how he moves his hand—west and east, right and left, as he rides his fingers on this brown field. It hurts to dream of him, his beautiful face and smile and laugh and voice. God, what would I give to photograph each moment of his existence and make my mind an album for his life! I could erase the past and let him rule over the room of my memory. I could love him until I get so weak in the knees and lose myself completely and be light like a feather so that my heart could be weighed in the after-life trial and get the pass to heaven—so that my life could be filled with joy and thunder and passion and sweet death and storm.

Everyday my mind sits in front of a blank paper holding a pencil to sketch the strategies to attack his image and flee his memory. But his name dances in my head. Each syllable moves wildly, unaware how every step leaves a fatal trail. And my lips keep remembering his kiss. I reproach them, but they won't listen. They cry out for his lips once and again and again and again. Do they think I am a hive they bees and him honey? And my eyes are starving. Who says people starve solely for food! People die everyday for longing. I get up in the morning and ride the tram to Stazioni Termini. He's got to take 105 to get to school. I wait. Cold and anxious. I wait for his appearance to bless my day, his smile to be my morning, his eyes my light, his words my faith. But he doesn't show up. My instincts fail me. The tricks life plays on us, letting us venture into a hot shower of emotions but then letting the water go cold and freezing the heart into a withered stick.

I've got to kill this feeling if I have to hire a hit man climb the heights of depth count the hundred steps to death hold my breath under the water descend from heaven a ladder see an exorcist a priest a shrink a Freud a movie consult a dead book a dead poet a dead painting a cadaver anything that'd rid me of this helplessness evoked by a cluster of malign-fingered feelings aiming at me and that'd halt these oceans of polluted tears storm-ing violent waves this sound of abrupt punctuations unresolved question marks unreliable commas irreversible periods this inerasable image of a face unlike any other eyes that have stolen my sanity given the heart legs shriveled pride and fear to a corner turned the leaves green crowned the

kingdom of thoughts with golden landscape of images lost do I live a-
wandering roaming and roaming in the round crystal of those two dark
ebonies. And as I wallow in this sea of emotions, I think how young I am;
how many more doors of opportunities are to be opened in the future.
This heart of mine will be a house of guests. Wide open and inviting. This
land will be ready to sow the seeds of love.

11

Suicide Machine

Smooth seas do not make skillful sailors

African proverb

ELISHEBA'S BACK WAS FULL OF CICATRICES, relics of cuts and wounds. Her legs confessed boldly their taste of fire. She had bitten more bullets than a hostage in his enemy's hands.

Meti, it's about to happen. He's coming for me, said Elisheba over the phone.

I immediately hung up the phone and ran upstairs, my heart pounding on my hands, knowing the significance of my mission. The look on her face had the air of hopelessness, and I could read weariness even from the way she opened the door. She invited me in, thanked me for coming, and walked me to her spaceless room. We sat facing each other. Before we had time to speak, the monster sneaked in the room and communicated in Tigriye with her, denying me the right to understand. I was giving him my back and I didn't care to turn to look at him, but Elisheba entreated me with a series of saccadic eye movements to look at him. And when I did look at him, he had his tongue out, writhing, anticipating the hands-on moment. He didn't see me looking, for his forty-and-more-years-old self was too busy making sexual advances to my fifteen-year-old friend. I turned to look at Elisheba, who seemed indifferent to it all. He left the room, but my desire to smother that motherfucker didn't leave with him and grew stronger in me. I got teary as I asked, *What happened?*

He was acting worse than ever today.

Did he . . . ?

No, she interrupted me, *I got away with an excuse and I called you. You know his coming at me and his doing me stuff is not new but this time I got so scared. I don't know why,* she concluded.

You don't know why? It's because it is scary, Eli.

But I'm used to it. I thought I was used to it. But I can't take it anymore.

· 109 ·

I sat there battling to pick the right words to say, but I was at a loss and I enraged at the realization that my hands were as tied as hers and I could do nothing except perpetuate the injustice.

I'd been always aware and clearly informed of the series of fiendish acts committed by the monster. I was her confidante. I was the one whom she asked what to do when she had enough of it. She wanted to run away to Genova where a month earlier she'd met a boy who taught her how to gain sexual gratification from eating a Popsicle. I objected her crazy idea and told her she was nuts if she thought that a fifteen-year-old boy would be willing to accept her with open arms and protect her from whatever she was running from. She said she had no choice.

What about the police? I suggested.

She said she couldn't go to the police for they would send her back to Africa and hell she didn't want that. And hell did I agree with that.

Then, what shall I do? she wanted to know.

I don't know, Eli.

Why don't you tell. . . .

Are you crazy? She wouldn't believe me and most likely she would put me on the next plane to Asmara.

I thought how telling the authorities or anybody at all was like turning her in, so I trembled from helplessness. We took a break from the decision making on this heavy subject and watched TV and ate instead. I said no more, for I knew words were useless, especially if they came from the robot that I was.

The same way spoiled food did when it lost its original taste, my life was losing its essence. At only the age of sixteen, I felt as though I had reached the peak of depression. I could smell the stench of melancholy all over me. Out of watching American movies and TV series, I'd thought sixteen was going to be sweet. I had thought that I was going to lose my virginity to a high-school sweetheart like Brenda did in *90210.* Or that someone was going to fall for me in place of Molly Ringwald and surprise me in the end of the beginning with a sixteen-candled cake. Instead, sixteen became a nightmare. Everything became meaningless. I was having emotional breakdown almost every day. I cried a lot. Complained and whined at the rhythm of the second. Then, one morning, I picked up a book from the library. It was an anthology of interviews made with patients who suffered from depression and an analysis of each patient by a psychologist. For about a week, the book made me feel good. I related to some of those depression junkies, and I told myself I wasn't alone. But afterward, I despised that book. I couldn't perceive how possibly a trained psychology graduate could enter and figure one's mind, translate someone's inner struggle in his own words.

It can be unforgivably cruel to equate one's country to a hell to be sent to if a wrong deed was done. I did everything possible to keep myself from being sent back to hell. I respected all the rules, which I'd have a hard time to translate into words since most of them consisted of figuring out moods, glances, and reproaches and acting according to them. But appearance was all I needed to keep me there. Because inside I was converting into a beast. My anger toward people and the world increased to an uncontrollable degree and couldn't be released for fear of being sent back to hell. I lied. I was mean to people. I became outrageously envious of my friends. I sat for hours brooding about grudges. I cultivated anger and overlooked guilt. I had the insolence of taking someone else's sweat. A voice said, *Meti, God forgives everything except those who steal and kill.* (Before, premarital sex used to be listed as well, but I supposed it wasn't necessary in this case). I already knew I was definitely excluded from God's favorite list, but being reduced to spend my afterlife in the pit where murderers were sent was a shocking revelation to me. I promised to God, if he still had any consideration for me, and to myself, that I'd walk on my knees if I had to in order to purge myself of all the filth that I had drenched myself into. I had long conversations with Maria Magdalena. She was my favorite. I had always had an affinity toward prostitutes; however, my obsession with Magdalena was beyond that. I was envious of her. Of her tears. She had used them to wet Jesus' feet. I prayed for the gift of her tears; to use them to get my forgiveness.

When the cheating drug was exorcised from my system, the craving for something to project my anger and frustration was still in me. And I found consolation in food. I ate until I felt sick. Then, I would watch movies about anorexic teenagers and dream to one day be like them. I became undeniably dependent on food. If I didn't eat every hour of the day, I felt nervous, and my thoughts were automatically connected to the refrigerators and the cabinets in the kitchen. Every week, I promised myself I would get off this habit of compulsive eating. I would start a diet on Monday but end it on Tuesday when my body failed to tolerate to be unfed. On Wednesday, I would feel guilty and decide that perhaps anorexia was not for me since I loved food and sweets so much. So I thought of trying to talk myself into becoming bulimic and that way I could eat as much fried food, pasta, pizza, croissants, chocolate, cookies, and ice cream as I liked. I went to the bathroom and put my finger in my throat, but I could not go through with it. There I was, a failure in making of myself either an anorexic or a bulimic. I saw no way out of my food dependence, and I thought of anorexia and bulimia as my only solutions to have a beautiful body. And I started to examine my body and my face feature by feature before the mirror. I despised the way I looked. I hated my high forehead, my slightly overbite teeth, my big-lidded eyes, my nappy hair, my big nose, my distorted legs, my fat stomach, my big breasts, my short height. I called clinics, inquiring information on how to transform my body.

How can I help you?

I need to know whether you offer the following services.

Si? Dimmi!

I want to get a hair implant on my forehead.

I want to get rid of my obvious eyelids.

I want a lift to my nose.

What else? Let me think . . . Oh, yeah, I want smaller breasts and straighter legs.

Do you offer all or any of these services?

Scusami, how old are you?

Sixteen.

You see, this will change when you grow older.

You mean that I'll grow hair on half of my forehead? My eyes, my nose, and my breasts will automatically shrink?

No. I mean that you'll change your mind and see things from a different perspective. You're too young now. All women go through this phase of dissatisfaction with their body and the way they look in general.

I tried to imagine Pamela Anderson and Cindy Crawford and all those goddesses on the covers of fashion magazines going through this phase, crying before a mirror as they looked at their perfectly sculpted bodies and finely painted faces, but the idea refused to salute my imagination. The woman on the line kept on talking, saying that the mirror would reflect a different image of myself in a few years from now without my having fixed a thing. It's all a matter of giving time a chance.

You don't dislike your body because something is wrong with it. You dislike it because of the way you feel about everything in general.

I had called a plastic surgeon so that he could make me beautiful. Not a psychologist to brainwash me. What did it matter anyway! Even if I had disregarded the receptionist's advice and chosen plastic surgery over self-acceptance, I didn't have the money to pay an overpaid plastic surgeon. Smart thinking as usual, Meti. Stupid on top of being ugly.

Mirror, mirror, on the wall! Who is the prettiest of them all?

The mirror is a tricky object. At times, the self-portrait enjoyed the self-service of its ego's nonverbal praise. But this time, the image it conveyed was unbearable. In fact, it was no longer an image. It was a message. It was no longer a self-portrait. It was the pointing fingers of million people repeating incongruous words. Ugly ugly ugly ugly.

The tears found repose on the corner of my mouth.

What happened outside my little introspective private world did not help at all. Racism showed its sharp tooth everywhere. At the post office, where I was on line, waiting, I felt dizzy and sat on the floor. But people did not bother to notice my trouble. Instead, they shouted at me to get up; who did I think I was to be sitting on my butt while they waited on their feet. They said that we *negri* had some nerve to think that we could come to their country and sit on the floor in the post office, letting them (the citizens) be on their feet. I did not say a word in response because I was in a transitional moment of my life, suspended between the exhaustion of strength and the conviction that I was an intruder in somebody else's country. So I went to a corner and sat until my eyes got over seeing everything blurry and my body quit feeling so weak. When I felt better, I called my friend Hebron to tell her about what happened. She understood me. I felt better. The scar was marked, but the incident was meant to end in the wastebasket of denial.

I watched my friends torture a cat and yelled at them to stop, but my shout was assassinated by their roaring laugh. So I just sat there, looking into the night, thinking how cruelly life played tricks on people. We were all converting into something we were not. We ditched school and sat inside the Big Burger, speculating about our future and dreams. I wanted to go to America to become an actress. Aaron dreamed of going to Amsterdam so that he could smoke marijuana freely. Joshua sipped on his wine and raised the carton as though his dreams were confined in there. If we were not strung out on our futile dreams, we were outside the burger place strung out on other futile things. We went to someone's house to cook *spaghetti alla svelta* and ate it from one big pot like animals, sitting on one another's laps. And I loved every little moment I spent with my dear friends, for I felt our bond was beyond the idea of camaraderie or solidarity. I had been as near as to hearing their hearts beat in moments like the time we went, full of enthusiasm, making the bus a madhouse, to say goodbye to Mishael, and came back carrying the story of a murder of our own fellow on our shoulders, our sullen mood this time transforming the bus into a funeral. I heard my boys' and girls' hearts beat fast, its sound highlighted by the silence surrounding us, and I felt my own heart come out of my chest. Because like them, I was aware that the story I had heard earlier that night about the boy who was burned alive was meant to be a warning. The fear of death bonded us. And it was that fear that instilled in us an instinct to be protective of one another. We were one another's guardians.

Meti, why aren't you at school?

Why aren't you at school?

Because this is what I do.

Drench yourself in the filthy water, lay your clothes on the ground for the sun to dry, lie on the grass and smoke pot?

Yup. But you're neither diving in the fountain nor smoking pot. You don't belong here. You belong in school.

Don't tell me where I belong or don't belong. I'm so sick of listening to you people lecture me. You live life like a movie, assuming the role of disenchanted youth. You're pathetic, you know that?

But Joshua has shut his eyes. He has followed the example of his friend, who was lying beside him, on a voyage to worlds foreign to me. The smell of marijuana had a melancholic effect on me. It made me nostalgic for authentic moments. It made me nostalgic for my friends whom I was losing, one by one, to an addiction. An opinion was formed. Never give your heart to a man with an addiction.

What are you thinking about?

The two of you.

What about us?

How long are you planning to live in this world?

Well, until I drop dead, I suppose.

No, idiota. I mean in this world you've created with marijuana.

It's no different from the one without.

Then, why are you so dependent on it?

Cuz it relaxes you, a term and a state of mind you're not very familiar with.

Why should you relax? You're fucking living in someone else's country and being treated less than you deserve. Who's gonna do your part for you in the real world if you're in Villa Borghese every day, relaxing?

I've no part to do in this place.

Then, why live?

Do you want me to die?

I want you to resist everything and everyone that tries to make you feel or tells you that you are anything less than extraordinary.

Joshua was my favorite person among the boys. I liked to watch him, study his movements. He walked lethargically. Spoke, stared, smiled, and even ate lethargically. He carried with him a carton of wine most of the days.

E il vino?

I am broke. I had to choose. Vino o canna?

How lovely!

He smiled and stroked my chin with his hand.

Then, a bitter day, years after the fountain incident, a phone call dressed my room in widow's weeds.

Joshua went crazy, Meti. I mean really crazy.

What do you mean really crazy?

He lost his mind. You missed his deterioration, Meti. You wouldn't have recognized him. He started acting very strange, and then he grew more and more violent. Once, he threw the dishes from the table at a dinner party that I had given. Just like that, out of blue. I could go on forever.

But he's always been a bit idiosyncratic.

No, Meti. It's more than that. He's no longer himself.

I wept myself to sleep that night.

12

The Trouble with the Feet

Don't spend the evening in a house
where you can't spend the night

Ethiopian proverb

THE ROAD TRIP TO FRANCE was the eerie calm before the storm. I was
miserable and had been so for months, perhaps years, and thought of the
trip as just another sham life created for me to participate in. I sat in the
back of the car and stared outside the window at the beautiful landscape.
I knew Sigmund Freud couldn't have had the answer to my state of mind.
And Matisse would not have been able to paint the stillness of my heart.
For all that mattered, I didn't know the cause of my unshakable sadness myself. Then, Paris appeared before me, more beautiful than a ballet dancer,
and something awakened in me. I was so struck in awe that I wanted to
run away and live on the street, feeding upon the breathtaking architecture and the sight of artists all over the city and the live lights at night and
the *bistros* and *cafés* and *monuments* and *jardins* and *rues* and *boulevards*.

*Meti, you go in the car. I'll bring you breakfast. I don't want them to suspect
we were one too many in there. We just paid for us.* That was more or less what
the voice said as I dug deeper into the ditch of explanations in my head for
why in God's name I was always chosen as the one who fit best in the soli-
tary corners of empty cars, charity houses, and loveless adolescence. I went
to and in the car while the rest enjoyed the comfort of hotel seats and terms
of endearment from obsequious servers. I looked past the glass and contemplated and at the same time ventured into oblivion. Breakfast was
brought. But it was useless to put food in my stomach. I was too far away
in my thoughts; too far away from this world; and too damn close to reality. We drove away, got lost, and eventually made it to the city. La Tour
D'Eiffel greeted me with her upright countenance. We went up a few floors.
I looked down and shuddered. How afraid I had always been of heights!

The old lady, I read once, was named after Gustave Eiffel, her creator.

She was 320 meters high, with 15,000 metal struts and two and a half million rivets. When she was built, in 1889, for the world exhibition to show the classical beauty of the eighteenth-century Ecole Militaire, some people, artists I believe, wrote petitions to have the tower destroyed. They claimed that her tall stature distorted the city's beauty. I thanked God for their failure to win her removal, for the moment I reached the upper floors and looked down, though I was intensely affected by vertigo, the view of Paris gripped my heart. From up there, the city of light exposed her beauty fully. From up there, the world seemed to be a better place, and life looked as if she was smiling at me.

The spell of peace of mind was yanked away from me when my feet touched the ground. And I paid only a cursory visit to the Place de la Bastille, the replica of Bartholdi's Statue of Liberty. Dome de Pantheon, the Carrousel arch, while I faked a series of smiles for the camera that captured the moment in front of the landmark and the historical monuments. As beautiful as Paris was, I couldn't get rid of the immense sadness that I felt and preferred to spend most of my vacation in the hotel room, rather than face light.

The journey continued into the exploration of more French cities. Between sleeping in hotel rooms and outside on benches, we got a piece of Bordeaux, Marseille, St. Tropez, Nice, Lourdes, and Monte Carlo. We stopped at the Spanish border, where *señorita* was all I heard in some strangers' endeavor to get past me or sell me something. And I longed for Paris, where at least my language skill got as far as *Je ne comprend pas le française, je m'excuse, s'il vous plaît.*

Thus I had set my feet on the site where the Virgin Mary had made her apparition to the shepherd. I had laid my eyes on the city where for centuries, artists, philosophers, and authors had created their best work. I had made love with the country where Descartes, Voltaire, Sartre, Matisse, and Dumas (*père et fils*) were from; where Picasso and Dali had found a home; where Jim Morrison was buried. I had left my footprints in the nation where the great *Dieudonné* Louis XIV was king for seventy-two years and where *le petit corporal* Napoleon ruled for a decade. Yet, I was sad and irritable. Sometimes, the most spectacular sites, moments, or chances seem nothing for those who see no discrepancy between prospect and retrospect and who have no concept whatsoever of present.

The sky had fallen. Down and hard. I couldn't live with myself, for my will was my worst enemy. And I couldn't abandon everything behind, for my will was my best friend. The whisperer, or perhaps I shall call it the shouter, broke the news in a cover-story manner the first time and in later days and months, squeezed the cover-page-worthy matter nonchalantly in the drool of cheap conversations. Find yourself a way (not a reason) to stay. But this was what I, the masochistic and between-the-lines reader, read: A reminder: You do not belong here. You never have. You never will. It was followed by a thoughtful suggestion that I should find either a family that would adopt me so that I would have more than a chance of obtaining a position in the long line of citizens awaiting naturalization. Or I should write petitions to persuade the Renaissance country to keep me. I was not sure whether I had to go knocking door to door, asking strangers if they wanted to adopt a sixteen-year-old girl, or use the overbite of my smile, dark complexion, and third-world features to lure old women at the bus stop into taking me under their wings. Neither knew I what contents my petitions should be packed with. The shouter commented rather indignantly that had I kept up my former ingeniousness, today I would have had quite a good reason to appeal for a *soggiorno*. Smart heads were sought after everywhere and always. Too old for adoption. Too stupid (damn vampires!) for acceptance (of any kind). Sixteen was too unprepared an age to learn that belongingness was not a given right if you were a fugitive in what you had come to believe to be a prophetic exodus. Then, where in God's name was the Promised Land, the land flowing with milk and honey?

The taste of my life kept getting more and more bitter. One evening, after an intense episode at the castle I was living in, I grabbed my backpack and left. I walked for hours, the time it took me to get over my crying. I got on a tram and the subway and went directly to Big. I ran into Joshua and his inseparable wine. He gave me some rational pep talk, telling me to go back home. Didn't like that idea. Fortunately, the only female present at that moment, Phinehas, didn't possess the same mind. She opened the doors of her home to me. Not knowing what was going to happen choked me to restlessness. At Big, I ran into Zipporah, who assured me that I had done the right thing and offered me to go to stay with her. But I resolved that Phinehas's was safer. That night, Phine and I decided to go to a party with the boys. Since there weren't enough scooters for everybody, they put Phine and me on the bus and agreed to meet us at the terminal. We arrived at our destination, got off the bus, and waited for them as planned. We waited for hours and no one showed up. It was deep night, and the place was isolated. Our friends never got there, so we got on the bus and went back to Big. We ran into Asher and an older friend of his, who took us to his apartment. They got themselves some weed, and Asher gave us a report on a book he was reading, entitled *Canna*. We left the apartment and went to the club. In the morning, Asher walked us to the bus stop and we went to Phine's home. The next morning, Eleazar called to tell us that the prior night one of the boys, Manasseh, had gotten into an accident and that he was now in a coma. That afternoon, it was like a funeral at Big. Everyone was worried for Manasseh. But the grief did not last long. And we were all smiles and cheers. But smiles and cheers are the best façade to cover the most brutal features. My body reacted strangely to everything. I felt sick. I felt closer to death than life. I stayed in bed for days and contemplated my entire life, from the beginning to the end. I was revolted by the images that ran in my head. I resolved that the world was a ready suicide machine and that my life was a sickness I nurtured thinking I was watering a fruitful seed. I was broken. But my feet refused to accept the fall. When you are in lack of a fairy godmother, you become one yourself. I started doing research on the so-called worlds people went to in pursuit of a better life. My friends were scattering over different lands. I asked the travelers what was it they were chasing after and they all had an answer: A Better Life. How did they know where to get it? Was it in the travel guide? Was there a map I didn't know about that indicated countries shaded in hot pink offered a better life? What was a better life? I didn't have to ask anymore. A better life was anything other than the filthy water I found myself choking on and drowning in. I didn't even know how to recover the life that I seemed to be on the verge of losing, let alone where to seek or how to go about finding a better one. What I knew was that I needed a lot more than some imaginary creature with magic power. Because there was only one thing that mattered in reality: MONEY. That is when you become a real fairy godmother and go seeking for the ticket to the flying horse that will take you to the Castle. I left Italy with a purchased passport. No goodbyes (for which I still get reproaches from friends), no big-time packing (what did God's people carry on their way out of Egypt to the land of the Canaanites?), no looking back (I certainly wasn't going to end up like Lot's wife). A single piece of luggage, and I kissed away Rome abruptly.

Book 4

THE BOOK OF
DISENCHANTMENTS

Come, make us a god who will be our leader;
as for the man Moses, who brought us out of the land of Egypt,
we do not know what has happened to him.

Exodus 32:1

THE LATE DECEMBER CHILL of a Roman evening had endowed my being with boredom. And solitude, in its darkest and shapeless suit, had reached the remotest corners of my soul. My mind, being unable to decide what conversation to engage in or which subject matter or philosophical quest to focus on, resolved to turn its undivided attention to the images and words that were simultaneously running on TV. I abandoned my company, which was composed of four young men, in their enjoyment of mutual conversation and *pandora/panettone* eating. I went closer to the TV and stretched my body across the sofabed and shut the voices of the boys behind me out. The news, *Notizia,* on *Canale 5,* was mostly eager to inform the audience on one specific phenomenon: Y2K. There were fewer than two days left to the year 2000, and the prophetic TV messenger was speculating about computer crashing and terrorist invasion. Yet, I could not pay attention to the warning of a possible scary turn of the century because Esu's presence was in the way of my concentration. I'd met Esu a week earlier at a Christmas party and liked him since. I was in Rome after an absence of four long years, and most of my first week had been invested in scheming tactics to conquer the latest object of my infatuation.

The boys left to get more food. Esu's body took the space beside mine on the sofabed. We borrowed the Y2K subject from the news and conversed about the possibilities of crashes and terrorism. In the meantime, I could feel my body grow tense. Somewhere down our conversation, his hands started to caress my neck, and then his lips invaded my neck and lips. He kissed me and kissed me until our tongues formed only one taste. His hands fished for any skin on my body, depriving me of my clothes. They undid my bra and found their way to my breasts. His mouth gently suckled on my nipples. He kissed his way down my body, pausing at my belly. And the entire time, I watched him in the fullness of his act, with my eyes wide open, analyzing his every move. He kept his eyes shut, and the look on his face had the air of someone who's taken flight. Again, he kissed his way back to my lips and again our tongues acquired the taste of one. I tried to participate by responding to his kisses and by running my hands through his dreadlocks, but nothing I did tuned me to the moment. Then, his hands unbuttoned my pants.

No, Esu. I've never done these things, I said.

Stai tranquilla! Don't worry!

His fingers entered the door of my vagina. It hurt. It hurt really bad.

Esu, it hurts. Aw, fa male, Esu.

He took his fingers out and returned to my lips and tongue and breasts and back to my lips. Then, his hand took mine and guided it to his penis and he let me shake hands with it and left me to my fate. I held it in my hand and did not know what to do with it. I was shocked at its erectness and dared not to stoop to look. Instead, I looked at Esu for direction. But he was in ecstasy and paid no attention to me. I freed my hand of the penis, still with no clue and no desire to do anything with it and forced myself to concentrate on the kisses. Only the clean kisses. But it was hard to do that, for his fingers were back down there, and it hurt like hell. I told him once again that I was hurting. He regained his fingers, and this time he used them to strip me of my underwear. I let him, but I panicked when I felt his erect penis on my belly.

No, Esu, no, I said. *I don't want to.*

He repeated, *Stai tranquilla!*

His penis brushed against my belly and I became terrified because I didn't know what it felt like when a man entered a woman and what if he was inside of me already. I closed my eyes to focus and make sure of the desertion of his penis from any reach of my vagina. I was relieved. Then, he endearingly ordered me to go down. *Va giù,* he said, and pushed my head in the direction of his phallus. My eyes ran into the factor that had threatened me the entire time. I made an effort to brush it lightly with my lips, smell it, and look at it. It had an eerie appearance. Its shape reminded me that of a fist in every sense of the word: it seemed to carry many a bad intention. I couldn't conceive of performing any act of union with such a violent object. I couldn't endure any longer the unclean feeling for coming so close, so tête-à-tête with my worst enemy of the night. I abruptly jumped my way up to kiss his belly and regressed to his lips to see if I could gain my innocence back. The boys were back, and I thanked God for His intervention. I told him I heard voices, and we both slipped into our clothes. The rest of the evening we acted as if nothing had happened; as if the prelude of seduction to intimacy, the caresses, the kisses, the uninvited lessons, the violation of the fingers had never taken place. I did not know what to think or feel or say. I felt dirty. And I searched for answers on Esu's pretty face. I stared at him questioningly, inquiring. He sat next to me, and I smelt his scent. I looked at his face and thought he was beautiful. I heard his voice and I forgot the disruptive intrusion of that experience. After all, I was walking away "intact." Nevertheless, once I was far away from it all, I wept tears of unknown origins.

13

Divine Detour

What is hanging up
cannot be reached sitting down.

Amara proverb

CALIFORNIA SMILED AT ME. I saw her straight white teeth and heard her clear ringing laughter through the windows of my imagination. The Los Angeles Airport looked very ordinary. Although my final destination was Vancouver, Canada; and Los Angeles was only a stop, a stepping-stone to the top, I enjoyed toying with dreams I had of L.A. The idea of her beauty danced for me. She undulated her belly, swung her hips right to left, tilting them up and down. She displayed her graceful handworks. And then, the dance came to a stop, and the music became a soundtrack to the faces that were facing me, attacking me, killing every sense of hope in me. I shuddered as I anticipated my journey and saw myself entering a world of unknown realities. The strange faces, the strange land, the strange language, and the strange customs overwhelmed me with a sense of fear and thrill. Life was once again opening the doors of possibilities to me. All I needed to do was to learn the tricks of the battlefield. I felt ready to go to war. I knew that if my sword was faith and it was aimed with courage, I would be triumphant. An alternative I had not.

The passport I was using belonged to an Ethiopian woman who was naturalized Canadian citizen. She was twenty-eight years old, so I dressed up like a grown-up to appear as close to that age as possible. I wore heavy makeup, a blue dress suit, and high-heeled shoes that betrayed my inexperience in wearing them, since I could barely walk. In Rome, I passed the board, but, in Los Angeles, where I was supposed to transfer to get to Vancouver, I was caught. I was sent to the immigration office. An officer received me and stared at me, detecting any resemblance between the picture on the passport and me. He spoke with the officer who sat across from him. They laughed, exchanged remarks, looking at me with their mocking and cold stares, and again they laughed, and I died to know the language they were speaking. One officer started at once to show and tell me, feature by feature, the sky-earth differences between the real woman, the lady on the picture, and the impostor, me. I couldn't understand a word he was saying, except the few nouns like *nose* and *mouth,* and from the way he pronounced them, I had a hard time understanding even those. He pointed out how my nose didn't look like hers, or the shape of my lips and my high cheekbones, and how much younger I looked. He showed me the picture on the passport, and I silently reproached myself for being that stupid, for the woman on the picture looked undeniably different from me. Moreover, she had on black shades. And the glasses I was wearing didn't look anything like hers. I used to give myself credit for being smart, but this episode would surely refute the impertinent assumption. But then again, what did a disenchanted sixteen-year-old on the verge of despair care about details! So I insisted I was the same person on the picture. Again, they laughed, and for the umpteenth time in my life I wished I were born in a first-world country so that I didn't have to be an orphan in other people's land and so that I could've spared myself from being humiliated one more time. He yelled I wasn't the woman on the picture. I whispered I was. I needed an interpreter. First, I asked for a French interpreter so that I could tell them I was from Quebec, Canada, but the French I learned in school ran for cover when the French-speaking flight attendant besieged my unfortified mind with words. Next, I was brought an Italian lass (notice my struggle to thwart a possible deportation to Ethiopia), whom I call angel No.1 in the city of angels. She sat there and bawled with me. The power of compassion and trust obliged me to reveal my identity. Enraged by the filthiness of a delayed truth and by my insolent lies that insulted their intelligence, the two officers bombed me with their fatal expressions and mouthing lips. The angel told me not to worry, that those men were mean and full of nonsense. They repeated they'd deport me to Ethiopia. She assured me they didn't have the power to do that, that everything would work out just right and I would remain in the United States. She said, *How about that, eh? Would you like to remain here and live with a new family?* I nodded and trembled with hope. My plan was not at all to come to Los Angeles. I was going to Vancouver and become a refugee in Canada. But there I was in the nation and the city of my dreams, and this angel sitting in front of me was telling me I had a chance to live there. Never in my life I had thought there could be a divine plan as intensely as I did at that moment. But fear always had a bigger grip on me and degraded my faith. I hoped and prayed that my fate in Los Angeles was God's will and asked myself time and again, *What if this is the way God has planned it and the tragedy would give birth to the amazing factor of staying in Los Angeles?!* After translating my answers to the questions the two mean-looking men were asking but especially after reassuring me to the fullest that everything was going to be fine and introducing me to an officer who seemed very sympathetic to me, to prove me that not everyone was against me, my God-sent angel left. I spent the rest of the night sitting in the office with the two mean men, listening to three Chinese boys cry incessantly, *Me no go back to China!* At dawn, they took our pictures, and we were handcuffed and taken to some other place. When I was leaving the airport, an Eritrean man who worked in the luggage department recognized me to be Ethiopian and slipped in my pocket a tiny paper. It was his phone number. One more angel act in the city of angels.

When we reached our next stop, I changed into a pair of jeans and a sweater. In the morning, we were taken to the immigration detention center in downtown L.A., where I spent the entire day. There, an officer, angel No. 3, who kept telling me I looked like Janet Jackson, interrogated me. And then I was taken to another officer, who asked me to choose between being deported back to Ethiopia and seeing a judge, or at least that was what I understood. This time, they put an Ethiopian interpreter on line. I asked him what to answer to some questions and he yelled at me that he was solely an interpreter and he was there to translate, not to give me answers. Of course, I chose to see a judge. The officer told me if that was the case I should know I would spend the time in a pretty rough place. Though I didn't know "rough" meant a juvenile jail, I asked her if I'd get beaten. She told me I wouldn't.

The lockup room I was taken to in the immigration detention center was full of Spanish-speaking women. Some of them kept saying *cara bonita* to me, and since in Italian *cara* means "dear," I couldn't understand why they named me or thought my name was *Bonita*. Months later, I was to learn that in Spanish, *cara* meant face and *bonita* meant pretty, and I was even more bewildered than I was the first time I heard the phrase because I'd always been convinced that the ugliness of my soul reflected fully on my face. That night, I was taken with a few other boys to my new home. A woman copied down all the information about me, sent to her by the officer who had interviewed me earlier that day, I supposed. Next, she bade me take off my earrings and bracelets. Then, she took me to the showers, ordered me to take my clothes off, checked my naked body, took away my clothes, and guided me to a stall to take a shower. Once I was done taking my shower, she checked again that I was the way I came out from my mother's womb, harmless. She gave me my uniform, yellow pants and white blouse, a bra and a pair of underwear. After I dressed in front of her, she walked me to the clinic. And during all that time, I was ignorant about my whereabouts. At the clinic, I was taken into a room, and a gracefully tall and plump nurse asked me questions. They got an Ethiopian interpreter on line and it was then that I found out where I was. The nurse asked what kind of a crime I had committed. And that, roughly translated in Amharic, was something even heavier. When I seemed not to understand the question, the interpreter made it easier for me by itemizing the names of various crimes: whether I killed someone or . . . My voice failed me, but I forced a determined "No" out of me. The nurse asked what was I doing in there. In my language, I knew only one word that wrapped up all kind of freedom-taking places, *Eser Bet* (Imprisoning House). I was stunned at hearing that word connected to the reason for my staying there. I corrected the misunderstanding by confessing that I was there for using someone else's passport. I grew extremely nervous and frightened after I found out I had just been detained. And the interpreter wasn't help at all. He scolded me for my outrageous ignorance, calling me illiterate when during the sight checkup I recited the letters A, B, C, D by pronouncing them in Italian. *You can't even say the alphabet! Where in the world do you come from?* Subsequent to that comment, I detested the mere sound of that insensitive man's voice and couldn't wait to have him off the phone. The checkup was over. I sat in the waiting room and watched TV with the other detained youngsters. It was scary, the experience of not understanding the language spoken. The words that people around me uttered fell like bombs from the high skies in my ears. The thoughts in my head jerked like popcorn chased by the wind. The popcorns were interrupted when someone came to get me. I was handcuffed and taken to a unit, the section where I would stay at for almost four months.

My bed was on the second floor of a bunk bed. I spent the entire night contemplating, looking past the glass and barred window out into the darkness, braiding my fringe to cover my high forehead. I watched the sun rise and began the first day of what was to be every day. Indeed, routine was the parent of that place. We were raised by it. That first morning, I didn't think I would stay in there for long. But the girls with more experience of the place assured me that there was a possibility; that they spent, some three months, others six. We spoke in the complicated tongue of signs. Later that day, I collect-called the man whose number I had been given at the airport. His brother told me how everything was meant to get used to. I told him not here. I was wrong. I did get used to it. But the battle to keep faith alive and not lose myself became invincible. I was sixteen years old, and I saw life falling apart like a broken-down building right before my eyes. I failed to find that precious bridge to connect me with anything that regarded faith. Once again, I was broken.

I knew that if I were deported, my life would have made no sense. I knew my only chance to make peace with life was to stay away from all that represented my past. I cried and cried. Prayed and prayed. Hoped and hoped. But despair dangled so noisily at the top of my head, I couldn't refuse to embrace her. I dreaded the day I'd be taken back. And at night, night terrors began bombarding me in my sleep. I can't recall a night I spent without having a bad dream. My days in Gehenna reappeared in visual metaphors. The Empress and His Excellency and their strict rules flooded my nights with scary scenery. The nights were better than the days because the days were endlessly infinite. The first weeks, especially, when I couldn't communicate with anybody, it was awful. But God's plan was accurately and cunningly arranged, for everything took place slowly. Although my inmates and I didn't share a language, we were still able to communicate. It is incredible what God is capable of when it comes down to unity. The building of the Wall of Babel was overlooked and the sins of the people forgiven. I became friends with Jahleel. Neither of us spoke English or had any language in common. She was from Mexico, and I promised myself that if I was to get deported, I would use the time in there to learn a language. I asked Jahleel to teach me Spanish. I found an English-Spanish and Spanish-English dictionary to check the spelling of each new word I was going to learn. Jahleel was a wonderful teacher. She taught me from the basics to have conversation and use profanities. She taught me songs by Selena. She wrote "Fotos y Recuerdos," "Como La Flor," "No Me Queda Mas," and "Amor Prohibido," and sang them to me, explaining each entire song, word by word. I would memorize each song and show up for the daily exam to sing it along with Jahleel and her friend Jahzeel. The listening comprehension took place in the laboratory of my bed. In the early afternoon, Jahleel would sit on the bed and recount to me the storyline of Central and South American soap operas. She narrated, like tales, stories about her little *travieso* brother and her childhood years in Michoacán and adventurous adolescence in Acapulco, where she hitched rides and to explain the word "lift," she stood up and posed, bending her right leg slightly and stretching her right hand forward. We watched a *telenovela* called *Lazos de Amor,* and every night I asked the meaning of those sentimental lines. I used to bug my teacher like a gadfly with questions. After two months, I was jamming in Spanish with my Spanish-speaking fellows. But besides teaching me Spanish and instilling in me the seed of her culture, Jahleel taught me how to survive in there. Only by watching her, I gained strength to go on. There she was, a fifteen-year-old girl, who had spent almost a year locked up, yet was full of hope and faith, claiming that God was her everything. She still knew how to dream. She kept getting my hopes high. She told me, *Mati, tu vas a salir. Vas a ver Los Ángeles. Vas hablar ingles perfectamente. Y iras a visitar el lugar donde se murió Selena. Vas a visitar sus tiendas. Y vas a comprar sus discos.* (You're gonna get out of here. You're gonna get to see L.A. You're gonna speak perfect English. And you're gonna visit the place where Selena died. You're gonna visit her boutiques. And you're gonna buy her albums.) I made friends with other Latino inmates. They all treated me as though I was a wanted guest in their circle. They shared with me their life experiences and their dirty jokes, with Pepito always as the protagonist. I inhaled a parcel of soul from different parts of Latin America. There was Izhar, from Nicaragua, with whom I had deep conversations on racism, war, and poverty. He recounted to me the bleak life he had led in Managua, and the hard time he had had in jail back in Mexico, where he tried to emigrate before he joined the expedition to the moon called the American Dream. Reuel, from El Salvador, who communicated with me with pure silence, smiled and shook his head each time he heard me speak Spanish. Ohad, from Honduras, whom I met in the van the day I was brought to the Juvenile Hall, never forgot to compliment me for being beautiful. Oholiah, from Mexico City, who narrated to me all about *su vida loca* in the city of the Aztecas, left her address with me, inviting me to visit her some day, in case my luck happened to differ from hers and I dodged deportation. Heber, from Guatemala, who was younger than most of us, asked me to marry him and run away together. And I laughed because it was his turn to run in the race competition we were having for fun and his *paisanos* shouted, *La migra, la migra,* and had him run faster. I fell in love with the Spanish language and the people who spoke it. They inspired me to see light from different angles while in the darkness. They caused me to laugh. *A carcajadas.*

Although Spanish was the only language I learned in the Juvenile Hall, it wasn't the only culture I got acquainted with. Chinese were an even larger group occupying those bunk beds. They too became part of me over time. They loved to sing. Day and night, they sang songs I had never heard before and did not comprehend. Their singing annoyed all the non-Chinese-speaking inmates. We told them to shut up, but they got right back to their singing. We got into fights all the time because their singing was in the way of our sleep and quiet conversations. Jahleel was particularly at war with them. One late afternoon, we were having dinner and Jahleel caught a word of their tonal language and she recognized it to be a curse according to their own translation. She called a staff member and told her she was being insulted. They said they didn't know what she was talking about. They were simply talking to each other. The staff turned to Jahleel and asked, *And let's hear, Jahleel, how would you know whether they were making fun of you or insulting you?* Jahleel answered, *Me understand Chinese.* The staff member smiled and shook her head and said, *Be quiet, Jahleel,* and left. Jahleel said to her supposed insulters, *Me know Chinese,* and we all laughed.

The sweet moments prevailed over the silly fights. Outside, we jumped rope in groups as our Chinese fellows sang Chinese traditional songs that fitted to the rhythm of the flight and the landing of our feet. And they had a great sense of humor and good hearts. With a few of them, I built a friendship that was as sweet as a juicy kiwi. We laughed together and assured one another. The bathroom was connected to the room, and I stayed a long time taking a bowel movement. Sithri pointed out with her broken English, *Meti, you too long in bathroom.* And they all laughed. I sat with them outside and teased them, saying how much they flirted with Mr. So and So. They would get the kind of upset that was a result of embarrassment. They'd repeat over and over, *No, dat no true.* And Sithri would get me by mentioning my too much time in the toilet. The girls were overly sensitive and cried more than I did. And when anybody cried, I was the one who composed sentences to console the weeping willow, preaching what I didn't practice, *Everrrytin' OK tomorrrow and blah, blah, blah. . . .*

The Chinese boys were wonderful people, too. Apparently, one of them liked me, so they always teased him and me about that. He told me every day that I was beautiful, which made me wonder whether that place blinded people. Once they were sitting segregated in a corner as usual. I joined them. The picture of myself among the many Chinese faces fed my heart with the beauty of diversity. Levi, whom I was very close to, was crying, and, as usual, I went over to comfort her. I made her laugh. Then, everyone, including the former crying lass, began chatting in Chinese. I could sense I was the center of their conversation. So I asked, *What he said? What she say? He said sometin' about me, huh!* Levi said, *You good. Me she cry, you always ask what wrong.* Levi took care of fattening my ego. There wasn't a day that she let pass without informing me and her friends, *Meti good!* The guy whom I teased for being one of the girls' boyfriend said, *You smart!* For he thought that my English was getting better very quick. And the guy who liked me said that I had beautiful eyes, to which compliment everyone else agreed, and then he asked me to marry him, and to that everyone cheered. I spent a lovely time getting compliments from these strangers, who were each leaving traces that read Levi has been here, Sithri has been here . . . on the sand of my life.

Ay Matilde, con todo eso de caminar, nos van a quitar lo poco de culo que tenemos, used to say Jahleel during our mandatory laps around the juvenile court. We both envied Selena's curvy behind and feared the consistent walking would deprive us of that feminine trait. We had to do several laps, and Jahleel and I walked next to each other, while she sang, *Matilde esta muy gorda—Matilde no la puedo cargar!* She called me Matilde because my name resembled the first four letters of that name and the song befitted me since I was always complaining about being fat.

Other than walking, jumping jacks and strict marching were mandatory. We marched in a queue, shouting after a leader, *Left—Left—Left, Right, Left*

(Left—Left—Left, Right, Left)
Cadence—Cadence: One
Can't hear you: Two
A little louder: Three
Much better: Four
Break it down: One, Two, Three, Four—XXX—Whoo! Whoo! Whoo!
Name of the unit: XXX
Name of the program: Blah. Blah. Blah.
> *Momma momma I can't see you*
> *Look what J.H. has done to me*
> *Took away my tennis shoes*
> *Now I am singing J.H. blues.*
XXX is the place to be
The other units wanna be like me

I miss my clothes I miss my skirt
When I go home I'll be as old as dirt.
> *If we don't mess up at all*
> *We just might get to make a phone call*
> *Keep this beat groovy*
> *So we can go in and watch a movie*

Every week, I was to go to court to see a judge in regard to my case. Three or four o'clock in the morning, the night shift staff woke me up, and after I washed my face, brushed my teeth, and slipped into my yellow pants and white blouse, I lined up outside with the rest of the inmates who, like me, had an appointment with the judge of their fate. They handcuffed us girls, but the boys were handcuffed and the shackles anchored to their feet. The van that drove us to our destination was skillfully fortified. Through its black bars, I stared outside at the city of angels. I prayed to God to some-day be free to walk those streets and wondered about the meaning of my journey, while the Chinese boys and girls gave background music to my wandering thoughts.

The room we were locked in until our time came to see the judge was awfully cold. We were given jackets, but that wasn't enough to appease our shivering bodies. The Chinese boys sang nostalgic songs from the next room, and their girls cried in the room I was in. I asked for the meaning of a couple of familiar words I caught amid the unintelligible lyrics. They told me one meant I love you and the other I miss you and they too joined the men in their singing attempts. But everybody was very tense, and the voices faded down as I observed the frail bodies against the wall and the shedding of tears. When we got back "home," Levi wrote a song for me in Chinese, in case I ever got to learn it. As hard as I tried to speak their language, I failed to master it. After many attempts to get the right tonality of the phrases I learned from my daily lessons with the songbirds, I threw the towel in and stayed with my newly acquired Spanish.

Every day, I lay on my bed and brooded over my situation. Jahleel worried about me and asked me what was that kept me so distracted and pensive.

Jahleel, how is America? I asked.

Ay, Matilde, Los Ángeles esta preciosa. Beverly Hills. Hollywood. The palm trees on Sunset. It is beautiful.

Then, she sat beside me on the bed and began her tale, which involved her friend's aunt, a brothel, youth prostitution, and betrayal. But she was so evasive, I wondered if it was the fate of us immigrants to be entangled in a labyrinth of shall I or shall I not, caused by a sense of distrust.

I spent my seventeenth birthday and Christmas and New Year's '96 at the Juvenile Hall. The free people came to visit us on the special holidays and sang,

> *Silent night—Holy night—All is calm—All is bright*
> *'Round yon Virgin Mother and Child—Holy infant—So tender and mild*
> *Sleep in heavenly peace—Sleep in heavenly peace*

And I slept in hellish tumult, waking up nine, ten times from horrid nightmares in which a few certain people were usually the antagonists.

> *Silent night—Holy night—Son of God—Love's pure light*

Jahleel and Jahzeel sang,

> *Feliz Navidad—Feliz Navidad—Y*
> *Prospero Año e Felicidad*

And I shuddered at just the thought of anticipating the New Year and all the things it was to bring.

We stood in a wide circle, inside the bedroom, against the wall, facing each other. We stripped our bodies of all garments except bra and underwear. The staff on duty bade us take the straps of our bras down, stoop, and shake our tits. Next, we were to open our legs wide, bend our knees slightly, take our underwear down a few inches and once again shake. And we shook like reeds to the wind, obediently. There are many forms of obedience, and the one that forces you to bend and shake is particularly attentive to show you the cruelties of existence. The girls, including the ones who appeared the toughest, couldn't thwart the tears from swimming in their sad eyes and diving onto their unmasked cheek. After it was made sure that no threatening objects had fallen from our hiding places, that we had not hidden a pencil or any other weapon with the help of either our vaginas or breasts to then use to put in danger someone else's or our life, we were ordered to put our clothes back on, and off to early dinner we went.

The ritual took place after our return from the one-room so-called school, where we had the opportunity to run into various edgy instruments. It was required of the staff to check us painstakingly. It was the part of the routine of the day that I dreaded the most and when I felt humiliated the most. More than the humiliation and self-pity, it was the picture of the seminaked goddesses around me that filled me with immense pain. Since I couldn't see myself, I looked into their eyes for explanation, and the mirror of the soul stabbed me with the truth of a bitter reality.

The judge, a Caucasian woman who, from day one, treated me wonderfully, after almost four months of incertitude in my heart, decided for my fate. I was granted asylum. I hugged the interpreter, cried, paid my respect to my God, and shouted, *Thank you so much,* to the judge, another angel in the city filled with angels.

14

Pandora's Box

The wasp says that several regular trips to a mud pit
enable it to build a house.

Ewe proverb

THE UNITED STATES OF AMERICA took me under her wings and lulled
me to rebirth. It was as if, for all the previous years, she'd held the core of
my existence a hostage. I got to California, and I found myself daring the
sky that before had looked unattainable. My dreams were set higher on the
winged streets of Los Angeles. The light of hope was switched on in the
charitable rooms of transitional housing programs for the homeless. My
soul-searching process began its root in the heart of this multicolored
haven. I was reborn in the generosity of this bighearted land and the kindness of her angel-filled city.

After leaving the Juvenile Hall, I began a journey that was to become
one of the hardest trials of my life. My faith was drawn to the edge of a cliff
and repetitively threatened. My great expectations were cruelly assassinated by a cold-blooded reality. My dreams of a better life and a place to
belong disintegrated at encountering the fact that no continent or country or city is the destination of our journey. That the top of the mountain
we strive to climb is not the mass of rocks and marble that face the sky but
the mere realization of self-understanding.

My first night as a free alien in Los Angeles was as exciting as it was petrifying. I was in the apartment of complete strangers, who were kind
enough to give me shelter. I spent part of the night wiping off the flood of
water that I accidentally caused to drain when I flushed the toilet twice.
It's curious how things repeat, for also in my early months in Rome, after
taking a bath at an acquaintance's apartment, the water flooded and an enraged tenant wiped off the floor. This time I had to wipe it myself. I concluded that the billow of water in a new beginning at a new place was a

sign of the flood of difficulties I was to come across. The toilet flood in
L.A. was an implicit warning: "Slippery road! You'd better roll your sleeves
and get the odds out of the way!"

Foreign feelings were aroused in me at my first contact, as a free non-
citizen, with Los Angeles. My hungry eyes were fed by the not so mes-
merizing aesthetics of the city that had been the home of my fantasies. The
first night, someone drove me to Beverly Hills, and I thought I was going
to choke of an overwhelming feeling. Every street, every house, and every
stranger had an effect of greatness on me. I was exhilarated and high on
life. I was proved for the first time in my life that nothing was impossible.
I was proved that God worked in mightily mysterious ways!

A program designed for homeless youth found me shelter in the house of
a Mexican family in the heart of Inglewood, California. The Capetillos
were an old married couple with ten children, of which three lived with
them. They were very old fashioned. They called me Mati, and every time
I went out, Señora Capetillo never forgot to tell me not to open my legs,
No abres tus piernas, Mati! I suppose that was her motherly way of pre-
venting me from showing up one day with a swollen belly. It was at their
home that I fell in love with Mexican food. *Quesadillas. Chile rellenos. En-
chiladas. Tamales. Carne asada. Mole. Sopes.* And, of course, the inseparable
moros con cristianos. Señora Capetillo poured her heart to me, reminiscing
about her youth years in Nayarit, Mexico, when she was free from worries
and the burdens of motherhood. She narrated in detail her hardships when
she and her husband came to the United States decades ago and shared one
room with their eight children and how she and Señor Capetillo had to starve
but always made sure their little ones had something in their stomachs.

Two rooms were built in place of the garage, and one of them was assigned to me. Two other girls occupied the remaining one. Lily was African
American, and Azucena was from Honduras. Lily was only a couple of
years older than I, but her overly thin body had borne and given birth to
two children. They had been placed in a foster home, and she was at the
time fighting in court for their custody. Azucena was a few months pregnant. She deftly hid her stomach under large-size T-shirts. *People don't
need to know,* she told me once. The father of the child had kicked her to
the curb right before the angel announced the news of the conception.

Lily and Azucena didn't get along, and I was caught in the middle, listening to each girl's complaints about the other. Azucena didn't like a bit
the inconsiderate behavior of her roommate, who disregarded the curfew

and came home late and interrupted Azucena's sleep. Lily accused Azucena of stealing the shoes she bought for her little girl. Azucena couldn't speak English and Lily did not speak Spanish, so I was their means of communication. The only time peace reigned between those two was when at night they both heard my incessant weeping that the thin walls betrayed and came together to my room to console me. Lily, in her salty Ebonics, and Azucena, in her sugary Spanish, reassured me that things would get better soon.

The worst part of my stay with the Capetillos was in the mornings, when at my awakening I'd find mice glued to the trap Señora Capetillo had set in my room the prior night. Mice ran around the room like legitimate children. I dreaded the day they would reach the territory of my body. Some mornings I'd sit on my bed and cry like a little kid, gazing at the mice twitching their tiny tails, struggling to free themselves from the trap.

Señora Capetillo and her husband had a little granddaughter who was diagnosed with cancer. I saw her dwindling gradually. Her days on earth were counted. Her body became thinner and took the shape of a skeleton. When I lifted her she felt as light as a feather. Her hair began to fall like leaves from a tree. Her big sunken eyes stared at me as though they were delivering a series of messages I wasn't meant to comprehend. Her pale cheek resting on my bare arm felt extremely warm. Her skin assumed the pale color of daylight in the presence of excessive snow. And thus I watched the beautiful flower lose its rosy color. I watched the petals fall one by one, slowly. The vivid bright color of spring entering the lovely breezes of summer nights only to lose it to the violent winds of autumn, and dead fell the leaves on the sterile ground and disappeared into the dust in the cold, rainy, lifeless winter.

I had just arrived from work that sour evening when I saw people gathering outside the house. I was told that Senora Capetillo's granddaughter had been in coma for hours and her death was expected anytime now. The angel lay still on the bed, her head in the arms of the suffering mother. I collected courage from remote places within me, and I went ahead to hold the girl's hands. I felt no sign of life in her tiny fingers and delicate palms. I gently caressed her face, patted the mother on the back, and stood in a corner looking at the weeping mother and her dying child. I too wept and trembled. I enfolded myself with my shaky hands to stop from shaking. I was ashamed that I couldn't censor my tears in front of the mother to whom I was supposed to restore courage with my strong countenance. It was around seven o'clock when I entered the room in which the little girl was saying goodbye to the world. It was two o'clock when I left the room, at señora Capetillo's suggestion that I had to get up at six in the morning the next day to go to work. I kissed the dying child's mother goodbye and left the sad house. When I entered my room, my heart failed me. I couldn't stop from shaking. I felt like throwing up, but nothing would come out. I sat on my bed and attempted to befriend a mouse, but it disappeared under the door. I got up from my bed and, as I was forcing myself into my pajamas, I heard a knock on the door. The mouse, I thought instinctively.

Mati, la niña se murió, announced Señor Capetillo's baritone voice.

I opened the door, and Señor Capetillo repeated his news. The little girl was dead. I insisted that it was not possible. For Heaven's sake, I was just with her and she was still alive. He explained that she died immediately after I walked out of the room. I ran to the house of the dead and saw the mother crying hopelessly and screaming for her daughter's return. She held the dead child tight in her arms. The child was pale white, dead still, and I literally felt my heart come out of my chest. My tears streamed down as if they flowed from a sea. I choked in my sobs, and my overly shaking body threatened my equilibrium. I went outside, sat on a strand of stair, and wept and inquired to God why he must take away life from a child like that. *Porque Dios tiene que quitarle la vida a una niña? Porque? Aaaahhhhh . . .*

15

The Boxer

The heart is not a knee, it does not bend.

Peul Proverb

THE BUZZ OF A FLY PIERCES MY EARS, weighing its insignificant existence on the scale of a mind already occupied by outrageous yet lethargic thoughts. I fix my gaze on the fast movements of the tiny insect until my eyes go dizzy. I could murder it with the violence of two clapping palms, but I choose to let it live. My decision is based on the sweet comfort of its company. (The mice have not been visiting much lately.) The house is empty. The family is gone somewhere to celebrate something. Oh, how I abhor festivities! My imaginary best friend is buried under the ground of my head, housing ants, making friends with particles of earth, contemplating why in the hell she chose a life of silence and peace over one of thunder and slaughter. She just got up and left one day, leaving me to face my cold reality alone, with no illusions to make things a little prettier. Sometimes, I wish I'd preceded her; who knows, perhaps, right now, we could be enjoying the mirth of the kingdom of ants and own their merrymaking with our busy eyes. But now it's too late. I'd missed my chance. I have yards of thoughts to cultivate and a best imaginary friend to avenge. Though, I must say that I haven't been the same ever since the adieu of my favorite friend. Illusion. Self-deception. But I am still here, in the room that I share exclusively with mice and cockroaches. I am lying on my loyal bed, mulling over heavy thoughts, trying to communicate with a loud insect, getting a point across, *Hey dude your life is in my fucking hands you'd better recognize and make an effort to loosen up your tongue if you have one or do whatever it takes to make this better because we're in lack of life here we need a sign any sign as long as it delivers life and life and life again and again.*

My time at the Capetillos was over. My case manager kept extending my stay to save me the humiliation of being stranded on the streets. It wasn't easy to find another place. I was eighteen, and most programs seemed to be willing to help only the group under this age. I could've visited a church and asked God for a hand but, lately, He and I had not been on the best of terms. So, instead, I visited the streets and parks of Los Angeles. I got lost in the dark avenues of my mind. Self-pity was my worst enemy. Yet, I seemed to be swimming in the dirty well of sorrow eternally. I couldn't stop crying. I couldn't cry myself to sleep. I couldn't sleep. I spent the nights memorizing the language of mice, gulping in the deafening silence of the night and fighting wars against infinite thoughts of no tomorrows.

As always, life surprised me when I least expected. My case manager found me a home. All I had to do was to go for an interview and endear myself to the interviewer with the sad story of my hopeless life. I passed the test. The sad story of my hopeless life won me a room at the Pie, a transitional housing program in Hollywood, a block away from the famous Hollywood Boulevard.

Living at the Pie was like living inside a boxing ring. It was an experience of a constant fight against the self. The day I moved in and greeted the building with no boxing gloves or gum shield, I was guided into an empty room that displayed a naked bed and a boring table beside a boring chair. I had one piece of luggage with me, and it held no trace of sheets or any adornment to help the room look a little more alive. I could lay my clothes across the mattress and oblige my Selena and Enrique Iglesias CDs to stand over the boring table, beside my ever-present stereo, I thought. That was what I was going to do for the rest of the day: play music nonstop. Music followed me everywhere I went the way my mother's scent did. I lay on the floor and faced the ceiling. Enrique Iglesias's *Trapecista* served as a background to my tears and the flood of self-pity I was drowning in. I too was on a trapeze. But, unlike the Spaniard's muse, I wasn't walking the dangerous road of love. I was walking the dangerous road of uncertainty. I sat up and faced the walls, the empty bed and the semi-dressed table. I looked over my belongings. I had a stereo, six CDs, an alarm clock that Señora Capetillo had given me, a pair of jeans, a pair of gray slacks, a few tops, a couple of sweaters, a brown jacket for winter, two pair of shoes, two bras, and some underwear. My whole life fitted into that bag, and it could not fill even a corner of that tiny room. Yet, I felt as though my heart were about to explode from overcapacity. And it was not love or hate or any other familiar feeling that I was loaded with. It was something I did not know what to make of, whom to give it to or how to manage it. My eighteen years of life had been a prelude to this moment of loneliness, reduced to an empty room and a lonely heart. I wiped my tears, grabbed my backpack, and left for school. I had to walk to Hollywood Boulevard to catch the bus. I was living a block away from the boulevard of my dreams and I was the unhappiest human being on earth.

Some girl who lives in this building killed her child and threw him in the trash, a stranger told me when I asked what all the fuss was about. The police invaded the place that I then called home, and they prohibited the right of way into the building.

But I live here! I said to the officer who was denying me the right to go in.

He told me to go around to the back of the building. Instead, I kept on walking down to Sunset Boulevard and into the movie theater. *G.I. Jane* was playing, and I sat there in oblivion. When I returned to the Pie, the girls were sitting in the TV room, watching a movie. We all acted as though nothing had happened. They were laughing and making comments on the movie. I got extremely irritated by their frivolous talk and expressed my irritation. One of them asked me what was wrong, and I said that what had happened that morning was immensely tragic and yet there we were going on with our lives. *I know,* they said. I felt like crying, but I couldn't. I felt like talking about the incident, but I could not do that, either. The girls spoke about the interview one of them had had for the news and about the night when I and, later on, another girl approached the baby, still alive on his mother's lap. I remembered his beautiful eyes looking at me. I asked the mother if I could hold him, but she bade me stay away from him and her. I shuddered when the girls mentioned the incident. I could still feel my hands against the baby's tiny hands. I could see his beautiful eyes looking at his surroundings aimlessly, and the rosy lips that had not yet formed a word. I couldn't bring myself to believe that a mother's hands had actually yanked her own child's life away. I was told that she had stabbed him, put him in a trash bag, and thrown him outside in the trash compartment where we all threw our trash. I felt some kind of worms growing in my stomach at the thought of her act. I didn't know whether the hole that those worms were digging inside of me was the pain that the child felt at having his life torn apart by the one who had given it to him or the inexplicable agony that the mother must have felt when taking away the life from a creature a few days after giving it to him.

India, my new case manager and my friend, was worried that I would never get out of my depression.

Meti, you'll go crazy if you keep locking yourself in your room all day.

She suggested that I go out to the beach, to the park, or anywhere where I could breathe fresh air and do fun stuff. Instead, I went out to get myself a job at my favorite place in L.A., the main public library. The purpose was to build a wall all around myself. The bricks were once again books. I couldn't think of anything that could be more fun than being banished from paradise with Milton or traveling in the pit of *Inferno,* the limbo of *Purgatorio,* and the heights of *Paradiso* with Dante. What could be more fun than finding out why the caged bird sings as Maya Angelou unravels the secrets of her childhood! What could be more fun than falling in love with a violinist ghost along with Anne Rice, walking the long walk to freedom with Mandela, getting beat up by slaveholders and attempting to escape with Frederick Douglass, or submerging my mind in the sweetest sermons by Martin Luther King Jr.? Thanks, but no to the beach and the parks and all that represented life. I had tried it before. Given up my books to venture into the world. What did it get me? An empty room and a lonely heart.

And then, there was Tuesday.

Did this room belong to Tuesday, by any chance? I had inquired the first time I was shown into my room.

How do you know about her?

I heard. I know someone who lives here.

They're not supposed to talk about it to outsiders. Anyway, we wouldn't be assigning her room to someone so soon after the tragedy.

Can you tell me which one was her room?

The room next to yours.

The room next to mine carried the story of a suicide. Tuesday hanged herself with sheets around her neck on the hinge of her room door. I was going to be her neighbor, but I came a few days late.

However, Tuesday didn't cease to be my neighbor even after her death. Tuesday lived with us. She walked in the hallways, stood by the elevator still waiting for Godot, appeared in the mirror, knocked on the doors, hid behind the TV set.

Oh, my God! Did y'all hear that?

Fuck! This place freaks me out.

Nights like this, I just want to sleep uninterruptedly. I feel like a child afraid of the dark.

Man, last night, when I was walking to my room after taking a shower, I swear I heard her. It was so real.

*Bullshit! Tuesday is dead, yo. There ain't no ghost walking in here or any-
where for God's sake.*

But we heard it again. The noise. Coming from nowhere. We were sitting in the hallway, by the public telephone. We were gathered like geese
on the surface of the water.

It's probably coming from the bathroom.

*Meti, the bathroom's door is closed. This noise was closer to us than us to
each other.*

Great! I am fucking living with a ghost. I grew up with vampires and
devils and now these girls are telling me that a ghost has moved in with us.
At least, the vampires and the devils had the reputation of being evil and
one didn't have to have any scruples to act against them. But I wouldn't
know how to deal with a ghost. She used to be among us. She knew those
girls better than I did. She lived in this place longer than I have. She probably knows me better than I know myself. Don't the dead have access to
everything and everyone?

Was she good friends with any of you?

Dalia raised her hand.

*We played cards a few nights before she committed suicide. She was a sullen
girl. She wrote dark poems. Beautiful dark poems.*

How old was she?

Nineteen.

And then, Kate arrived.

*It's Tuesday's ghost that makes her act this way. She lives in her room. She
must feel her presence every second of the day.*

The girls speculated, trying to find an explanation for Kate's heavy
mood and pessimistic view of life.

Can we leave Tuesday out of this for once? She's dead, guys.

Meti, you don't understand. This place is haunted.

I don't believe in that shit.

Then, why did you run downstairs the night of Thanksgiving?

It may have been a thief.

A thief my ass. That was a ghost.

We were watching a Quentin Tarantino film, *Jackie Brown*, the night of
Thanksgiving, when we heard it. The noise. We locked the door to the TV
room, turned off the movie, and waited in silence.

We should throw things out of the window. Maybe someone will notice us.

We could throw the books.

What if she enters from the window?

I never heard of a flying ghost.
We threw the books, emptying the shelf that we used to block the door in case the ghost tried to outsmart us and use her preternatural strength to get through. *Don't ghosts disregard doors and pass right through?* I had inquired. But I was told that it was safer to block the door because we were expecting not only ghosts but also intruders from earth.

No one noticed the books flying from the sky or heard the hard fall to the ground.

We should call out her name. The receptionist's.
We screamed the receptionist's name in unison. She was out of sight, at the front door. No answer.

Fuck! We're done.

We gotta get the hella outta here.
Kate grabbed a chair. Songbird armed herself with a book. I led the way empty-handed. I had my back covered by my brave girls. We took small steps, making sure there were no surprises coming from the empty rooms and the empty corners. Suddenly, we stopped dead. It had come from the bathroom. We were sure.

Holy shit!

OK, girls. We gonna run like we're running for our life. Ready? One, two, three.
We reached the elevator in matter of seconds. The receptionist had not seen or heard the slightest attempt on our part to get her attention. We called the police. As we waited, we looked for signs of intruders through the monitor that they had downstairs to check on us when we were in the hallways. A janitor from the gym walked in on our state of fear, and we were relieved by the idea of having a man with us. We told him the story. But he made matters worse by revealing to us how only a moment ago he had been outside and seen someone standing by the window upstairs, on our floor. Holy shit! The three of us were the only losers who spent Thanksgiving night watching a rented movie. Our fear was confirmed. We had had a visitor. The police arrived. They searched the place. No ghost was seen. No living person was found. They scolded us with their glances. For wasting their time, I suppose. Although I felt certain that the man had lied about the figure standing by the window, I could not convince myself that the visitation was merely in our head.

An admission to a transitional housing program required a few mandatory visits to the free clinics. The first trip was for TB and HIV test. The clinic was in Beverly Hills. The second trip was for a drug test. The clinic was in the neighborhood. I went with the mother of the most beautiful little blonde girl I had ever seen. I thought it was a perfect time to ask her what was her relationship with the lead singer from the Red Hot Chili Peppers. He had been seen at the Pie the day he came to pick her up.

Oh, yeah! I know him from the rehab days.

Rehab days? What kinda days are those? asked an ignorance named Meti. The mother told me about the battle against her dependence on heroin and how the hardest part of the fight was with the cravings not of the body but of the mind.

So Anthony was at the rehabilitation center with you or something?

No, no. The group has been clean for a while. They like to do support stuff now. He took me to a meeting the day he came by the Pie. That's where the addicts go.

I'm an addict. Hi, my name is Meti and I am a CocaColaholic.

A few years after the drug conversation, the mother of the beautiful girl let me listen to a song by Red Hot Chili Peppers and told me that it was about her daughter, the most beautiful little blonde girl who'd grown into an even more beautiful big girl.

The third trip to the clinic was where I thought I lost my virginity. It was a complete physical check-up. The nurses took my blood. I peed in a plastic cup. A woman took a tour around my breast, and popped the question. Was I sexually active?

No.

Have you ever been?

No.

The doctor put on the gloves and reached for pointy objects.

What are you going to do?

It's called a Pap smear, and she explained to me what it was.

Will it hurt?

Not really. But you will feel uncomfortable.

How uncomfortable?

You will be fine.

If fine was feeling like something pierced right through and took the life out of me, then, I supposed I was fine.

Am I bleeding?

Just a bit. It's normal.

The doctor and her assistant were women and when I looked up I caught them staring at me with a look that revealed that I had much to learn from life.

We're all done, said one of them.

I walked the forty-five minutes back to the Pie. I asked the girls what did they know about Pap smears. They wanted to know what I was interested in that for. Virgins don't take Pap. Did I have a virgin label on my forehead? Girl, don't need to. You know a real virgin by the way she walks. The next day, I was walking strange all right.

Be quiet, Meti! You can't lose your virginity in doctors' hands in a clinic room.

You call that clinic room? India, I've never opened my legs that wide except the time with the doctors at the Juvenile but it didn't hurt at all then and they didn't spend so much time down there.

Meti, you did not lose your virginity. That was a Pap smear. All women must have it. Grow up!

Wasn't it enough growing up to live in a strange land, with no family, and to have to go to bed hungry on days the number on the paycheck was too low due to the days missed from work? Anyhow, who needed growing up when there was Woody Allen in his ever neurotic roles show the world how the older you got the less satisfied you became. On our way to 20/20 to rent *Annie Hall,* Songbird told me a joke she had heard on *Saturday Night Live,* but I didn't get it.

Meti, it's funny. She gets her protein from his thing.

She eats his penis? Don't they call that cannibalism?

No, Meti. What do women do with a penis?

They have sex.

What else?

They do . . . how do you say it in English? The sucking and the pulling?

Blow job.

They call it a job? I was thinking more in gastronomic terms.

That's with the women.

The women? Please, don't tell me we've something designed for pulling and sucking! Last time I checked, nothing was hanging.

Meti!! Nothing is hanging. That's the reason why they eat you out.

Eat you out? Fuck! There is a world of language and feast and jobs that I never even heard of, let alone been part of. How am I supposed to catch up?

Start with the joke that I am telling you. She performs a job and gets protein.

The yellow stuff . . . eew! That's not funny!

I was silent for a long time, formulating questions.

So, one has to swallow it?

Not necessarily. You can also spit it out.

That means it will get in your mouth one way or the other.

Well, when he comes, you can also take it to the sheets or to the floor.

Sex looks good, but this protein business just sounds gross and unappetizing.
Did I devote so much time to fiction and movies to live a life of delusions?
Sex was supposed to be this immaculate picture of two people moving to
a rhythm no choreographer would have found the steps to. It was supposed to be a private and graceful dance that the man led on top and the
woman followed from the bottom. It was supposed to be music played by
the ear not the mouth.

I squeezed my eyes shut and opened them again. It was real. They were
kissing. And yes, the lips of the party of two belonged to girls. I had heard,
talked about lesbians, but I had always been under the conviction that it
was a legend, pure fiction and television.

*The girls seem to turn gay after residing here. The Pie has the lesbian
epidemic.*

Lily, who, like me, had moved from the Capetillos to the seemingly
lesbian-infested house, was in my room telling me the gossip. Songbird
had told me how loud the girl next door was when she had sex with her
girlfriend. How was that possible? A girl could not have sex with another
girl. I had seen them try it in those porn flicks, but they always seemed to
be resorting to unnatural methods. It was necessary to have a slightly long,
narrow, bottle-shaped piece of flesh to enter the mortise that hid behind
the black bush, wasn't it?

No, Meti. You've just never been exposed to it.

*Things I can't imagine myself doing are being with a woman and giving up
Coke, chocolate, and meat. Is that homophobic?*

No. But the Pie might blend the homo and the hetero as one in your head.

The homo and the hetero did blend, just not in my head but at the gay
and lesbian center where the guy whom Tamara, a resident at the Pie,
wished me to meet lived.

Meti, please! He is cute and sweet and it's love at first sight.

He lives at the gay and lesbian center!

I lived there. It's a transitional housing program. Just like the Pie.

Before I knew it, I was spending my evenings outside the gay and lesbian center, listening to Tamara's friend tell me about his turbulent childhood and his future dreams, sporadically interrupting himself to point out
things that involved digging.

Look, Meti! I think she digs you. A lot of them do. You should see them gather by the monitor whenever you're downstairs buzzing for me. They be digging you.

Digging! That's a new term.

Are you attracted to girls at all?

If I were, I wouldn't be here talking to you but up there by the monitor digging.

While the girls upstairs did the digging, the girl outside was supposed to be hugging the boy.

What is it with the hugging in America? What, am I supposed to hug every guy I talk to? If they need affection so bad, why don't they go to their mamas?!

He finally told you.

He discussed it with you like it's a problem?

Meti, you gotta show the brothers that you're interested.

Isn't listening to them for hours enough?

You gotta hug them.

Is that the L.A. dating system?

That's the human dating system. Touching.

I was on Tamara's bed, eating Chinese and listening to Erykah Badu sing about Tyrone.

You got a date?

Yup. Do I look cute?

You look hoochie momma cute. Who is he?

It ain't a he. It's a she.

When did you start going out with girls?

I always have.

But you had a boyfriend.

And I still do. I'm just having fun with her. They call it bisexual in America.

They call it cheating where I come from.

Meti, when was the last time you had sex? Don't you ever get horny?

I swear if I hear that word one more time . . .

How well do you know the Puerto Rican guy who works at the corner store? You like him?

No.

He's no good for you, Meti.

Who are you to give me advice on men? You've a boyfriend and are going out with another girl behind his back.

He just did time.

Really? How do you know?

I just do. And it ain't just that. You deserve someone more like you.

Who? Our friend at the gay and lesbian center?

Our friend from the gay and lesbian center and his hugging business were just too much of a cross to bear. I needed a new target, and the Puerto Rican man at the convenience store seemed the perfect resort.

The next day at the library, I asked a coworker who knew a lot about men from prison whether she knew anything about finding out information on ex-convicts.

There is a number you can call to find out what crime they committed.

She wrote down the number on a piece of paper and told me that I needed his last name.

I still had not found out his last name or the crime he had committed when the ex-con asked me out to dinner. But the date he chose was New Year's Eve, and I didn't want to leave Kate home alone on a holiday.

What if he never asks again? I asked one of the front desk receptionists at the Pie.

I've been telling you, Meti, but you don't listen. Men are too complicated. You should turn to girls. You'll love it. I speak from experience.

No, thanks! I'll deal with the complications.

But it was not the ex-con who turned out to be complicated. It was me.

If you're not planning to have sex with the guy, there's no point starting anything at all. Everything leads to sex, said my friend Semay.

But sex is a potential child and I'm not into abortions. Are you telling me that unless I change my principles about sex, I have no hope to be in a relationship?

I am just saying that sex is a big part of it. Especially here in America. When men flirt with you, they don't think kisses and light petting. Their mind is elsewhere.

That night I looked up the word "horny." And I realized that in order to experience the word, I had to completely shed from my skin the importance of symbols. But I was not ready to feel wet. I wouldn't have known where to start. I also liked and was too attached to the sense of dry that my thoughts produced.

The men Meti loves. The title of my first book, said Kate between brushing her teeth and spitting out toothpaste and saliva in the sink. Meanwhile, I could be seen in the bathroom mirror sticking my head out of the window.

I could serenade him a Mariachi song. I could ask my Mexican buddies from the Boulevard to be the band. I've a better idea. Billie Holiday. I sang, "I Must Have That Man."

If they gave recognition to people who've no voice, I'd rise to stardom overnight.

Meti, you're cuckoo. First of all, you don't serenade standing on the third floor to someone who is on the ground floor. It should be the other way around. And I've never heard of a woman serenading a man. You're just bored and you want something to keep your mind busy. That's perfectly fine. But no serenading!

Kate was right. What seemed to be a syndrome of a chronic "desperately seeking romance" behavior was in reality a desperate search to put a stop to the ever-swinging pendulum of boredom.

I never did serenade the guy. Not because I lacked the courage but because I lacked the voice. And when I was on my way to see Napoleon for a consultation on a new strategy to a successful conquest, I realized that I had had a change of heart. A different man was underneath the bathroom window folding towels.

You did what? Kate wanted to know.

I had to. The guy disappeared. Poof! Like a ghost. He was no longer downstairs folding towels and looking after the kid.

How did you get his number?

I asked my friend the janitor whom I knew had connection.

And what did you say to him when you called?

That I had some questions about handicapped kids for a research project and that since he worked with them he could help me. The man wanted to answer the questions right away and get it over with on the phone so I had to come up with a reason to see him. That was when I thought of a paper to show him. And after we agreed on the time to meet, I hung up and ran to my room to come up with a story.

You weren't even interested in the guy until he was out of sight. It's not him you like. You like the challenge and the work that you have to put into in order to get to him. What is wrong with me? I thought. Was I sick? Was I so bored? Or was I lonely? And if so, why couldn't I stick to a one-man-plan and get in a damn relationship and at once see for myself what was this phenomenon everybody was raving about?

The Christian fanatic Salvadoran woman who baby-sat my friend's children said the answer to all my questions was Jesus Christ.

De verdad, Meti! How many times did we have this talk? You have too many question marks in your life. You need Christ.

Can we not disturb Christ for once? It's just a stupid guy pattern.

I resolved to convert my very last infatuation, whom I got to see with the pretext of a research project, into a healthy, long-term relationship. I left the door open a crack. We shared opinions, dreams, drinks, and poetry. And then one day . . .

Have you ever been kidnapped?

No. And I'm sure it has its charming elements but I've a psychology test worth twenty percent of my grade tomorrow morning so I should be in my room studying, soon.

You don't understand. You don't get a say. On the contrary, you're in danger.

He was driving down Hollywood Boulevard.

When was the last time you watched the stars?

About a week ago at a movie premiere outside the Mann Chinese.

That's why you need to be kidnapped. Too much Hollywood. You need some nonfiction in your life. Maybe I'll take you to Palmdale to show you the real stars.

Well, I should inform the real stars that I've a curfew and if I don't respect it . . .

You'll get a strike. You already have one, two more and you're out.

Who told you about the strikes?

I have my sources.

We were in Los Feliz.

Hah! What else did your sources tell you?

That you're a little cuckoo. That you're a disaster in the kitchen. That you caused the alarm to go off many times by burning bagels in the toaster and blowing up the microwave. That you love Coke and chocolate but for everything else, you've a wall.

Did I just hear him say that? Where was this wall everybody seemed to be running into when it was built in such a way even I never noticed it near me?

You don't even look at me when I talk to you.

What I looked at was Griffith Park. He drove through the park, and I hoped he would go up to the crowded Observatory. But he parked his car nowhere near it, and we were, as I feared, in a secluded island. And when I turned to look in his beautiful green/hazel eyes, I saw his toddler son and his ex, and when he made a move to kiss me, I had already pieced the picture together and decided against the kiss.

Don't you think Griffith Park is bit too open to be bringing your kidnap victims?

You're the boss. You don't want no kissing, then, no kissing.

He never took me to Palmdale to show me the stars that night. The next conversation we had was over the phone. He asked me how my love life was and I told him I didn't have one and wasn't interested in one.

Then, what are you doing with me?

I am making friends.

What are you going to do with all these friends once you've made them?

Friends are never too many.

They are if one of them happens to want to be more than just friends.

That was the last time we talked. This time I was the one to disappear. And he never got creative enough to write a paper and have a friend the janitor to help him reach me.

Kate did not deny the presence of the ghost in her room and its influence on her mood. But she did not blame her suicidal thoughts on Tuesday. She blamed it on life.

Life loves to sneak in on you and lead you to self-destruction. One moment you're happy and the next you're trying hard not to do away with yourself. You're still fresh, Meti, so be careful not to get fucked by this life. Don't let her sneak in on you. Be wary!

Kate, you're as fresh as anybody else, whatever it is you mean by fresh, so stop talking like that.

I am just tired of this crap. Living is a fucking chore. Worse than the chore we do here at the Pie. At least, here, someone signs off on our card so that we can prove that we did our part. I have been living for nearly thirty years and no one seems to sign any card that shows that I've done my part.

Of course, someone has. You're still here and you've turned out to be a beautiful person. I mean that in every way.

It doesn't matter if you're beautiful inside or out. I don't know what it takes to live anymore.

But you're alive and you're doing a pretty good job with yourself.

Meti, this isn't living. This is death. I am homeless. I am jaded. I am nobody.

It was an upscale party at a castle in the Hollywood Hills. The organizer of the party needed doormen to check in the guests. But once my friend and I were dropped off at the castle, my help was no longer needed. The party was divided in three parts. The VIP room in the back required a code made up of a sentence that made no sense to get in. The large room with alcohol and dancing people offered men with hands that elongated into ass-biting snakes. The courtyard was decorated with corners that hosted couples having sex. I found an empty corner and colonized it to look in the view of my beloved L.A. I was joined by a group of strangers, who said that I must've been the youngest person at the party. Was I wearing a prom dress? Was I drinking red wine? The wine didn't do it for them anymore. Was I Ethiopian? Did I know that Ethiopians were considered to be the most beautiful people in the world? Cheekbones to die for, lovely eyes, and long necks. My skin so naked. No foundation. When was the last time they left the house with a naked face?

I went to the VIP room to join my friend. Curtains separated the room into three sections. From my seat, I had a view to the gambling room where men played at cards or sat in a circle, impatiently waiting to receive a lap dance from the seminaked woman who moved from chair to chair rocking her body on top of sweating men who buried their faces in the cushion of two flesh-made pillows. A curtain led into another room where I could hear a tape that played duets. It was an uninterrupted score of moaning. Apparently, in the gambling room, the head found so much comfort in the cushions and the crotch grew so fond of the warm thighs enfolding it that there was no other choice but to take business to the next room where the head would be free to move from the cushions to the roof of the thighs and the crotch to the ceiling that shouldered the cushions and thus draw the number 69 as a warm-up position to tune the strings for the upcoming concert. One more place in the world where I don't belong, I thought, and called a yellow cab and went back to the Pie.

The Girls and the Men

Girl #1

Once upon a time in America, a woman and a man made love and as a result the woman gave birth to a tiny baby with hazel skin and a distinct laughter. The tiny baby grew to be an extraordinary woman. There was in the woman with hazel skin and distinct laughter a strength that overwhelmed an outsider's comprehension. It was beyond anyone's capability to understand how this petite woman could stand tall against all odds and observe the world's misfortunes with a silence that suggested wise resignation. It was the kind of resignation that knew thoroughly the pros and cons of a fight and had chosen to take a road like no other. It was the kind of resignation encountered only at the end of a Calvary, and no cross feels heavier than the one just carried. The sighs and silences that resignation gave out opened in me a sense of hunger for the past of the girl who had apparently walked in my life many years after the Good Friday.

Let us go back to the woman and the man who made love and created the child. One heartbreaking day, that same man decided to possess the child with hazel skin and distinct laughter in such a way only men with sick minds can. The father raped the child also known as his daughter with extraordinary strength. Was a child conceived as a result? Maybe. Was the child with hazel skin and distinct laughter that I saw crying as he parted from his mother and got on the car with his foster parent the result of that obscene act? I didn't know. Was the lack of tears and the unblinking countenance of the storyteller when telling me the story the result of that obscene act? I was sure. Was the old man that I was being introduced to and shaking hands with a repentant father? It seemed so. Had the woman who was smiling at me and helping the old man rise from the chair forgiven him? She had. Was the daughter the same person she was before the obscene act? I think not.

Girl #2

I heard a knock on my door. I was sharing an apartment with an aspiring actress in Hollywood at the time. I wasn't expecting anyone, so I was curious to know who was showing up without announcing his or her visit over the phone. I opened the door and the face of darkness greeted me. The visitor had placed one hand over my eyes and the other hand over my mouth. I went to sleep for what seemed to be an eternity. When I woke up, my entire body ached, and I saw everything blurry. I was in my apartment. I took a shower, dressed, and left for work. I worked for an acting agency. When I got to work, everybody stared at me with horror but didn't say a word. Once the staring subsided, my boss wanted to know where I had been all this time. He said I had not shown up to work for over a week. I laughed in disbelief or perhaps thinking that he was telling a joke. But he wasn't. I told him I had left work only yesterday, gone home, slept, awakened in the morning, and taken a shower, and there I was again at work. Not missed even a day of work, let alone a week. He had been scrutinizing my face while I talked. He said my roommate was worried. I had been missing from my apartment for over a week, as well. I couldn't be found anywhere. He wanted to know who did this to me. His teary eyes were taking a tour around my face. I went to the restroom, and I met the elephant man in the mirror. I never found out what happened. My memory completely erased the episode. Meti, ever since, life has been a subject I have a hard time digesting. Human is a cruel race.

When the storyteller was done with her story, I excused myself and ran to the bathroom to release the tears.

Girl #3

In the late twentieth century, somewhere in St. Louis, Missouri, a tall and graceful young woman dreamed to become a musician. She would some-day move to Hollywood, California, make a demo tape, and send it to various music managers. She would walk to Capitol Records and see if she could get a job doing something, anything, as long as it would allow her to have one foot in. After all, wasn't Aretha Franklin or one of those divas doing the dusting and the sweeping and the mopping when a producer heard her sing and signed her? Did I know that Diane Warren had an office down the street from the Pie? "Because You Loved Me" for Celine Dion, "Un-Break My Heart" for Toni Braxton, and God knew how many more hits she'd written. How great would it be to find out her secret to song-writing? All it took in the music world was one hit song and after that you were fixed for life. In the meantime, she would teach herself to play the keyboard, write songs, and carry the notes as high and as long as possible. However, in between her dreams for the future and her present, an inci-dent took place and marked her life forever. Before the incident came be-tween her future and her present, a man had come between the dreamer and her mother. The man disregarded that a family was already settled in the house when he came along. He didn't respect the dreamer's individu-ality and, most of all, her space. So, one heartbreaking day, he invaded that space and threw an object that was either on fire or just hot enough to burn the dreamer's face badly. The heat, the pain, the humiliation, the fear, gradually faded. But the scar, internal and external, could not be erased. The fire was permanently lying across the dreamer's cheeks like the mov-ing ridges of the ocean's waves. The fire was also evident in her response whenever I complained that I wished to belong in this city, in this world: *Everybody belongs!*

And then the men came.

Kate and I were watching Thursday night black comedy. Kate loved Steve Harvey and the Wayans brothers. She wanted to marry Damon. The night shift staff interrupted us. Would Kate please come out to the hallway? Then I heard the voice of a man. It was eerie to hear a man's voice coming from the corridor at night. We were not used to male visitors, and even the janitors did not come around at night. Something crept like a many-legged insect inside me. It must be the man's voice, I thought. But the creepy feeling would not leave me. The voices in the corridor were fading. I left the TV room, and when I reached the long hallway, I barely caught the sight of Kate's handcuffed hands making a turn at the end of the corridor. My heart sank inside an unknown ocean. My legs followed the heart. I squatted and held my head down to let the blood rush back to my head. I ran barefoot to the elevator. When I got downstairs, the receptionist asked me if I was OK. I looked frightened. Through the glass door, I could see Kate standing with a few men. The men did not wear uniforms. I pushed the glass door open. I had tears in my eyes. Kate smiled at me and said that everything was going to be fine.

What's going on? What happened?

Nothing. I'll explain everything to you later. I left a message for you with the residential counselor. Don't worry! I will be fine.

A man grabbed her elbow to walk her to a car. So this is how we lose people, I thought to myself. They are handcuffed and taken away from us in the darkness. The message she had left for me with the residential counselor concerned her belongings. She wanted me to put everything in storage. I was not revealed any more information.

The next morning I received a call. The caller wanted to know whether I was willing to bail Kate out. I said I would think about it. Later that morning, I sat in the office of the Pie's executive director, facing the executive director, my case manager, India, and another friend of Kate's. The friend confessed about Kate's frequent spacing out. I confessed about her suicide talks. Why didn't I say this before? I said I did not want a team of men wearing white outfits to walk in her room and take her away. But look what happened instead! Then, I presented my dilemma. Shall I bail her out?

With what money?

The woman on the phone said I didn't have to show the money. I just needed to sign a statement and, true, a large amount of money is involved but it's just on paper and I don't have to provide it unless . . . But I don't even know anymore if I know her well, look what happened, to be sure that, you know, I won't have to pay it later cuz she will, you know, not reappear in court. . . .

I was talking like a madwoman.

Meti, you're not even twenty-one. You're homeless and practically an orphan in this country. You can't make this kind of decision.

India, she's my friend.

Doesn't she have family? asked the executive director.

Well, she gave Meti's name as reference, not a family member.

Meti, no way!
They didn't have to say it. They'd already helped me make up my mind. I was not going to sign the paper. So this is how we wash our hands clean, I thought.

No one was left on my floor. Tuesday had committed suicide. Kate had been arrested. Songbird had gone back to Texas. The rest had left the place to move on with their lives. What was I to do? I lay on my bed and gathered my thoughts and squeezed them so hard that too many ideas came out of it. I could always go to Miami, Florida, and mingle with the flood of Latinos and try my luck in the Latin music industry. Or I could stay here and let things take their course and if I was lucky I could come out of this mess clean. I cried and cried. Wrote a long letter to God, listing the symptoms of my inquietudes. I left my room and walked on Hollywood Boulevard and reminisced about the time I had taken those very routes with the people now making their exodus, some perhaps on the final one and others, God knew to where. And I claimed to know the meaning of it all. The meaning of meeting people and parting from them. The meaning of suicide, murder, and natural death. The meaning of existence. I was tired of living my entire life, choking on my own tears, which seemed to derive from a deep sea secluded in the depths of my soul. I was tired of being helpless whenever those dear or not dear to me hit their heads on the wall of destruction. Was I to live my entire life idly as my brothers and sisters hanged themselves, got arrested, or were stabbed to death? What use was I to this world if my idea of better life was success and prosperity? Was I not guilty of the crime of wanting to be somebody? What about everybody else? Those newborns abandoned outside my house haunted my memory. And the children who couldn't afford to go to school so they made the shade under the tree by Shuni's house their learning center. And my mother and the lifetime death row she was condemned to. What was the point of complaining if the hand was not raised when called upon?! I collect-called my girl Rebekah in Las Vegas. She agreed to come pick me up. I went to my room and wrote a letter to God in which I declared that I had chosen Vegas as my next destination.

The Strip hadn't changed a bit since the last time I visited. The lights were charming and the sidewalks were full of people as usual. Bellagio was transported from Italy. If my memory does not fail me, Paris was on her way. The old lady was still young, but the technological ladder in the States moved so fast that in the blink of an eye a whole town seemed to have been built. I had been several times in Vegas, and each time I had left it with a growing desire to never come back. But things had to be, and there I was again in the city where people traveled to fulfill their dreams of avarice.

A nail clipper is a multipurpose object. I fixed my eyes on the sharp edge of the tiny silver knife that stuck out of the nail clipper. I didn't know whether it was from my lifetime-lasting obsessive fear of rape, but the little sharp knife reminded me of a penis standing out from a man's body. The man holding the metallic penis in his hands and waving it at me was not a complete stranger. I was introduced to him a few days ago at a casino, had seen him at Circus Circus the night the old Egyptian man took Rebekah and me out to see a show and he'd spent this evening with us. He was now sitting on the passenger seat, drunk. Another man was sitting by my side in the backseat. Rebekah was driving them home. The street we were on was empty. The time was night. The reason the drunken man had to resort to his nail clipper was that I'd offended him. I was very conscious of the derisory words I'd used. They were meant to hurt him. I could not stomach his behavior, and I wanted to tell him so and did it with craft, utilizing all the subtle ways that life had taught me and, on many occasions, used against me.

You think you're better than me, eh?! said the angry man.

Put that thing down, baleghe, sid, said Rebekah.

He ranted about my character and called me names. He grew veins on his forehead. His eyes wished to shed tears, but he seemed ambivalent to grant them their wish. I stared at the metallic penis with a contained countenance. I was scared, true, but I was also tired. In the space of ten minutes or less, I had evaluated my life. The system had stopped working for me long ago, and did this man want to jab his metallic penis right through my throat and end my misery, may he be welcome. But those theories did not form until later. They were simply evident in the sense of my balanced fear. The drunken man popped the metallic penis back in the nail clipper and got out of the car. The man sitting beside me, who was drunk, too, didn't want to follow him, so Rebekah and I dragged him out of the car. Rebekah and I went back to her apartment. She went to the bedroom to sleep. I stayed in the living room and philosophized some more on the meaning of my life. If all the sacrifices, all the changes of identities, all the transformations of the self, all the fucking suffering by my mother, me, and everyone involved in this crime of living came down to the simple act of a drunken man and his metallic penis, then, so be it. It was then that I heard the knock on the door. It was three o'clock in the morning, for fucksake. It was the man who shared the back seat with me earlier that night. His voice sounded like the crackling background of a static-y old record. I turned the TV on and raised the volume all the way up. An episode from the past show of my life flashed back to memory. The vampire screaming alcohol-ridden words and I turning the stereo on and blasting the volume. I had thought I was done dealing with vampires. The consistent, lazy knock on the door drove me crazy. The reason I had hurt his friend earlier with words was that he'd thought he could talk to me any way he wanted to. How was this different? He had been knocking on the door for over two hours, speaking unintelligible words, and, true, none of them referred to me, and his visit wasn't intended for me, either. But I was the only person lending an ear to his noises. Don't drunken men doze off into sleep? Life, I will give you one more chance, and if you keep insisting that I was indeed born to face dilemmas, "Shall I let him in or not?" "Shall I get out of the car or stay?" "Shall I bail her out or not?" "Shall I speak up or keep quiet?" "Shall I lie, or will the truth be just fine?" then, my darling, we have a problem. I believe you've had your laughing long enough, now it's my turn, even if I get to do it just for a minute, I'm gonna say what I've been holding back all my life, and afterward, whatever happens, happens.

I sat at the bar with Rebekah and her friends, but I was asked to leave the bar unless I showed my ID and it read "twenty-one." The bartender said I looked fifteen. I was twenty, thank you very much! I went looking for a job and failed the interviews, mostly because of my age, too young to serve alcohol or work in a place where one has to deal with gambling machines, which equated to everywhere. Rebekah said that she believed I wasn't getting any job because of my red braids. But then I got a call from a casino for a waitress position. Again, my age was an obstacle, so the manager offered me the busboy position. I took it. I was hired immediately. They bade me change the color of my hair. I did. I wiped and set the tables. I took turns in being a runner and pushed the cart loaded with piles of dishes to the dishwasher. I lasted a week. The turning point came when I was getting ready to leave for my job one afternoon, and a Grammy nominee came on VH1 and endeared herself to me with dreams-come-true stories. I called the casino and told them that I was quitting. Effort for survival was necessary, I thought, but that didn't mean I had to completely deviate from my path, which included neither Las Vegas, a place swarming with the things I craved to be free from the most, nor a job that I took just because I had no choice. Life needed to be harassed in order for one to find her kernel, and that was exactly what I set out to do. Harass life till I peeled all the rinds and got to her kernel.

16

The Dancer

Who digs the well should not be refused water
Swahili proverb

THE EXOTIC DANCERS LOOKED absolutely gorgeous in the fancy underwear showing excess skin on their perfectly sculpted bodies. They moved with so much agility, grace, and confidence around the silver pole on the round stage that I wondered whether performers were born with self-esteem foreign to ordinary people. The audience was losing its reason to the goddess who seemed to be making love to the metal pole. When her hands traveled across her skin, the men comprehended the act to be a message. Everybody knew the language spoken on the stage by the seminaked woman. Her hand touching herself, or spanking the derriere that was facing the hypnotized faces, her breasts shaking with a little help from the shoulders, her tongue stirring like a spoon around her mouth. . . . However, backstage, it was a different scene. I did not find the strippers memorizing vocabulary to speak the body language fluently. They were desperately seeking what I learned to be their true self-esteem. In that chaos of cravings and underwear changing, while behind the curtain the men were sizzling like hot oil on a frying pot crying for more meat, the goddesses remembered to introduce themselves and paid my smile a compliment.

When I was a teenager, in Rome, I once had a front-row privilege to see a male stripper get down on one hand and stick the shaft into the faces of his ululating fans who stuck *lire* bills inside the vault that held the gem. However, the men in the audience at the strip club in the Valley in California were not amateurs devoting the night to the dancer. The men seemed to have lost the use of their senses and let the ruling member run their life for them.

I was at the strip club with my supervisor from work, who happened to be friends with one of the beauties. It was in that backstage little room that I realized that, no matter how well we might think we have read a book, we are never really able to judge it any better than we did when we first saw the cover.

The angels who gave me shelter during my days out of the Juvenile Hall, a married Ethiopian couple, had come to my rescue again when I left Vegas for L.A; I had stayed in their home while I looked for a job and found employment at the Natural History Museum. A gallery interpreter. Traveled back to prehistory. Hung out with the bones of dinosaurs and live snakes. Memorized names of gems. Build a relationship with butterflies and moths. Saved money. Moved into a studio. Went back to community college. Happy for a while. But the fall didn't wait long.

Prozac was the solution to all my problems, or, at least, that was what the supervisor who gave me the first taste of the world of women strippers suggested.

It does wonders, Meti, she said.

Wonders were the moods that I went in and out of. My boss at the museum wanted to know what happened to the girl she had hired. Where had all the enthusiasm gone? There had been a report by the weekend supervisor that I dragged with me an eternal sadness. My Italian buddy from a film class said I had converted into a tree. Ethiopian living in a Palms version of *Siddhartha,* he specified. He pointed at every tree in Santa Monica as he drove down Ocean and asked me if I recognized any family member. Did I want him to park the car so that I could reunite with my family the trees? My neighbors taped a paper to my door and the letter contained a drawing of a Buddha and their wish to be present when I jumped off the Bay Bridge since earlier I had expressed my eagerness to know where the hell did all the suicide junkies get the courage to end it. Why was I clinging high water and hell to this world? Why was he clinging high water and hell to the girl? asked a coworker, interrupting my long train of thought and taking me away from my company misery. Why had she dumped him? He wanted to know. We both agreed that Jose Cuervo would have some answers, and after work, he drove to Ralph's to pick J.C. up and take it to his apartment, where we finished the bottle, taking shots with salt and tapatio in a therapeutic session, singing the lyrics to songs we never heard of, except . . .

> *Todos me dicen la negra llorona*
> *Negra pero cariñosa*
> *Yo soy como el chile verde*
> *Picante pero sabrosa*

. . . drinking a toast to him, " The hell with her!" and to me, " The hell with life!" until I passed out on the floor and woke up on the porch in front of a pool of vomit. Let me take you home, offered the cousin of the friend, I don't know you, I don't trust you, said I, You can sleep in my room, I'll sleep on the couch, offered the friend, I choose not to sleep in a house full of boys, I wanna go home now, said I, and stumbled my way to the car. The friend and I ventured off on a wild ride on the 10, headed west . . .

> *Dicen que no tengo duelo llorona*
> *Porque no me ven llorar*
> *Hay muertos que no hacen ruido llorona*
> *Y es mas grande en su penar*

My friends displayed faces that inquired as to why I was not resorting to African proverbs, quotes, songs, books, and anecdotes from past experiences to solve their problems. Why was I summarizing their burdens in a single "That's life!" wrap? Where has Meti gone?

Meti had gone cuckoo, spending the nights outside wrapped in a *gabi,* gazing at the moon for hours, staring at herself in the mirror in a diligent bargain for tears that never came, cleaning out her closet and her drawers of most belongings, letting the phone ring nonstop as if the sound were music to the ears, counting the number of knocks on her door without making a move from the bed to open it, walking down Vermont, Venice, and National barefoot, holding her shoes and ignoring the running cars and their sudden halting and the insistent honking and what was she on a suicide trip? the drivers wanted to know, and following the young man down Los Angeles in Downtown, with eyes shut, wishing him to be a brave murderer and would he please turn around and shoot her. . . .

I am sick of school. I am sick of working. I am sick of everybody. Everything is so meaningless. I have no kindred spirits but the authors and composers that I never met and will never meet in my life. I see no possibility of a like-minded companion. I am alone. I don't even have myself. I have lost me because I am chasing after things that make no sense to me. Fuck getting a degree! All I do at lectures is write stories and poems. I can teach myself anything. I don't need someone else to train me to speak a language or to think about the books I read.

All this I complained on the phone to my friend Bela, who seemed to be the only person who understood me. But she lived in Italy, and the phone calls were too expensive. So I found myself a shrink for free.

Pas de Deux

Dear God, this is a lament. The twenty-five-cent burrito diet ain't working for me no more. Just the sight of it makes me run to the sink. The solution would be finding a job and buying decent food. But you seem to
be shaking your head at this suggestion of mine. Then, what do you say,
habibi? I don't know if it was your idea, but I have been smoking cigarettes,
lately. It takes the hunger away. The smell is terrible, though. My hair, my
clothes, my sheets, and even my skin have incorporated the tobacco as part
of their immobile existence. I know you blame me for it all. Irresponsible
me. Quit my stable job and spend my savings on a trip I couldn't afford.
But the truth is that I'm not to blame. My feet are the ones to blame. They
itch badly if I stay too long in one place. It's a disorder that I have. Inherited directly from you, I think, cuz no family member has ever had trouble
with his feet. *Habibi,* I was told there is no cure to this. Am I supposed to
go on for the rest of my life wandering like a vagabond with nothing to fall
back on but Albertson's twenty-five-cent burritos and appetite-stifling free
cigarettes from pedestrians? By the way, thank you, love! My trip was amazing. Loved New York. I don't think you approved of her so much, since
you screwed up every attempt from my part to settle in the East Village.
What's up with all this interfering? You really wanted me to acquire a taste
for these beef burritos, didn't you? Let me tell you a little more about my
trip. Toronto did not like me at all. She refused to smile at me. I made an
effort to befriend Queen Street, to steal fleeting moments from strangers'
lives on Yonge and Bloor, but no luck. All I got was a frown. I can't blame
you for that, cuz I didn't hang out much with you up there. I was kinda
doing my thing, you know. From Canada, I took the greyhound to D.C.
The capital reminded me of home. She was swarming with Ethiopians. I
heard Amharic right and left. Smelled *wet* on every corner of 18th Street.
Next stop: Boston. Gotta love Boston. So old, so mellow. So many universities and even more young people. Spent lots of time on the water in
Boston. After so many museums in D.C., I guess I needed a break from
fossils and artifacts. I went whale watching and was enthralled by those extraordinary sea mammals. They are acrobats from another world. They
moved in and out of the water so freely and, oh, with so much grace. I also
went sailing with a group of strangers, and an elderly lady had the insolence to tell me that it was inconceivable to live in a place without seasons.
If snow up to your knees and twelve pieces of clothing from head to toe
(winter, they call it) or endless winds dragging you from right to left and

slapping your naked face with the violence of a cold air (fall, they call this one) is the definition of season, then the hell with seasons (excuse my language, but it was necessary to make my point). This lady obviously has no appreciation for year-round sun. However, L.A. isn't filtering her sunny days into my place (which won't be mine for long if I don't find a job). She is rather grabbing me by the neck. Every morning, I have to come up with brilliant arguments to persuade myself to get out of the bed and apply for one more job. You think there would be reward for my efforts, but, no, instead I've to deal with phony interviews for stupid jobs. What do they think this is? A contest for the Nobel Prize? Anybody can be a salesperson. I wasn't born to put on a fake smile and repeat a prefabricated line to sell a product. *Habibi,* help me out, here! You can't entice me with a box of chocolate and then lock me in a waiting room with a bowl of broccoli. You can't promise me a tasty life and then feed me pure vegetables. Love, may I ask one thing of you, though? No matter what, stick around, cuz I enjoy your company. Without you, my heart is a spineless invertebrate.

You were lost, so you went looking for somebody to find you, said Semay, when I told her I was seeing a therapist.

She was right. I saw therapy as my last chance to run into myself and make sense of my life. Dr. Brillantini greeted me cheerfully, and, after he offered me a seat, he politely asked me what was I there for.

I am here for different reasons. I have all these disorganized thoughts wandering inside my head, I began my tale. *I dissect everything. I question things. And the whys are driving me crazy. People around me are constantly telling me that I will go nuts if I keep on living like this.*

So you're mentally disorganized, he said.

If you want to put it in those terms.

Give me an example, he asked.

I am reading Mein Kampf *by Adolf Hitler. Well, Hitler, who, as everyone knows, committed some atrocious things upon the human race, speaks of God with as much passion as any devoted believer would. For years, I had related my unconditional belief in God to the production of love and being a good human being. I spent this entire weekend pondering the question, What makes me think that bragging about God means I believe in love and in being good if someone like Hitler preaches God's name with as much conviction as I did? I used to feel special for believing in God, but now I feel that my belief is degraded. If someone like Hitler feels connected to God, I may as well consider my faith as ordinary and attainable as a cheap fantasy.*

Dr. Brillantini's beady eyes stared at me enigmatically. I could see right through him. He had already identified me with a specific group of his patients. He had already found answers for me in one of his psychological books.

OK. Tell me what are the other reasons?

My dreams. I have nightmares everyday. A friend of mine told me the other morning that I was whimpering while sleeping and my hands were fighting against the vacant space. I lived in transitional housing a couple of years ago and the girl who lived in the room next to mine used to bang on the wall in the middle of the night and ask me if I was all right because she'd heard me screaming. Every morning, I wake up with a heavy, numb feeling in my head. And most of the time, I can't remember my dreams.

What else? asked Dr. Brillantini as he nodded to acknowledge that he was indeed listening to me.

I feel lonely, I complained. *Really lonely. I feel tired. Not physically. But I am here mostly because I can't remember one large phase of my life. Most of my childhood years have abandoned my memory. The strange thing is that I do remember the ordinary stuff. It's the traumatic events that I cannot recall. Even when someone else reminds me of a specific episode, the scene comes back to me in fragments or not at all. It's as if I lost part of my memory.*

I see, said the psychologist, as he obliged the neurotransmitters in his brain to extract information from that part of his brain where years of study had been stored.

Are you dating anyone? he asked.

No. Why?

Is it a choice?

I guess, I said not knowing what he meant.

Is there any other thing you would like to say?

No.

I am glad you came here, Meti. Next week, we will pick an issue in your life and start working on that. In the meantime, I want to ask you to jot down your dreams. When you go to sleep at night, put a pen and a piece of paper by your bed and the moment you wake up, write down whatever you can remember about the dream you had. I promise you I'll help you the best I can to get through your issues.

I looked at him suspiciously and I asked him boldly, *No offense, but I just want to understand what is it that you have that can help me. What makes you think, as a psychologist, you have what it takes to help people? I know I'm here because I evidently thought of you to be my last resort, but I honestly don't know the reason beyond it.*

Well, he said, raising his eyebrows. *This is my profession. I studied psychology for years, read hundreds of books on the human psyche, earned a Ph.D., dealt with many patients, whom I hope I was able to help. And I assure you that we'll get to the bottom of your story.*

Tex-Mex

Meti, shiiit!

The shit that Songbird was screaming about was the shitty-looking water I jumped in with my clothes on. It was deep night and we had just arrived to Corpus Christi, Texas, and as our first stop I had my friend drive me to Selena's statue. The statue was by the water and since prior to the trip I had spent some time in Houston, where the most exciting thing in the city was to walk up and down Westheimer, jumping in the water in Corpus was as good as it got. But then, I couldn't get back out and Songbird couldn't help me because she was on the floor laughing and letting go of my hand every time she attempted to pull me out of the water. Even though there was nothing amusing about having my legs invaded by tickling things and hurting my toes as I was trying to climb up the wall out of the water, I too joined my friend in her laughing. Finally, we both could control our convulsion and my feet touched the pavement. My clothes were drenched not just with the filth from the water but also with the pee that I let out while laughing at myself. My toe was bleeding. We drove in the city, jamming Eminem and Bob Marley. The next day we went to the cemetery to visit Selena's gravestone and later to the studio where she recorded her songs. Her father, Abraham Quintanilla, looked intimidating at first but turned out to be quite charming. I told him how I was introduced to his daughter's music after her death during my early days in the States. He took me and Songbird on a tour around the studio. He showed us the room where Selena recorded her songs and introduced me to the man who wrote one of Selena's hits and showed us a piece from a video to be put on sale soon. The video was toward the ending and when the credits came, he noticed that his daughter's name didn't appear as one of the composers for "Bidi Bidi Bom Bom." The man who was preparing the video said he didn't know.

Yeah, Selena too composed the song, said Selena's father, proudly.

Yeah, I remember seeing her name on the credits for the song on the Amor Prohibido *CD,* said I.

You see, even she knows, said Selena's father.

That was all I needed from Corpus Christi, a piece of Selena to take with me.

Selena wasn't the only celebrity we hunted after. A week earlier, we were in New Orleans inspecting the house of Songbird's love, Nine Inch Nails' Trent Reznor, and buzzing for Anne Rice.

Yes?

I am here to see Anne Rice.

Mrs. Rice isn't here. May I take a message?

Could you tell her Meti dropped by? And that I loved her ghosts and vampires.

When I had given up to the idea that Texas had absolutely nothing for me except the fact that one of my best friends, Songbird, lived there, we entered San Antonio. It was a breath of fresh air after a long period of suffocation. It was a beautiful city with fine architecture and an even finer nightlife. We couldn't find a cheap motel, so we decided to change in the car and go out. Songbird said she wanted to make a short movie to show her friend, Chris, who was supposed to be on this trip with us, what he had missed. What he had missed and was now being filmed was, first of all, Meti fixing her boobs, which were practically falling out of the bra, Meti pulling up her blue jeans and showing off the back of her thong and ass. Songbird asked me to talk to the camera as I put on eyeliner.

I'm gonna walk to a good-looking stranger and kiss him.

And I'm gonna film it.

But there were no good-looking strangers around, so we walked on the San Antonio Riverwalk instead and then went to Fat Tuesday, where I got so wasted that I could've sworn I was flying and not walking on our way out of the bar. I saw a good-looking man standing in a corner. I had to stumble down a few strands of stairs to get to him.

Would you like to kiss me?

I sure would.

That's my friend Songbird up there and she's gonna have to film us kissing.

No. No filming.

Then, no kissing. But it was very nice meeting you. Bye!

I walked down the streets of San Antonio screaming and when we reached the car I ran to the back to pee and Songbird ran after me to film that too.

We hopped in the car and I was still screaming and the cameraman was driving and filming and showing me the potential kissers walking on the street. I felt sick so I asked my friend to stop the car. I passed out on the ground in someone's front yard. Songbird was screaming about the police when I woke up and saw her filming. That was the last thing I remembered of San Antonio. I woke up in the car in a parking lot somewhere in Texas with the worst hangover I've ever had and a swollen toe as a souvenir from my night in Corpus.

Meti wants to see cowboys, said Songbird to Chris over the cell phone. We were driving in Songbird's hometown, Houston, searching for cowboys. We spotted out a bar that had a couple of them. A country song came on and an old man with a trucker hat asked me to a dance but the way he had checked me out when I walked in the bar made him undesirable for a dance partner. Back in the suburbs, Songbird put me behind the wheel and I drove us straight onto the sidewalk.

I didn't scribble down my dreams like he asked me to for the next time I went to see Dr. Brillantini. However, I resolved to share a couple of dreams I had had a while back that seemed perfect subjects for an analytical interpretation. But before I began to tell my tale, Dr. Brillantini wanted to know what was the book that was lying on my backpack.

The Portrait of the Artist as a Young Man.

Is it good?

Very very good.

Who is it by?

James Joyce.

I've never heard of him.

He's Irish. He writes in stream of consciousness. I'm not sure, but he may be the inventor of that style of writing.

What is the book about?

It's a semi-autobiography of the writer. Catholic upbringing, the guilty feelings, the search for selfhood.

Can I see it?

I handed him the book. He read the title aloud, read the back of the book, and twitched his face.

Interesting, he concluded. *Did you write down your dreams?*

No. But I'd like to share with you a couple of dreams that I had a while ago. Go ahead!

Once, I dreamt I was raped by someone whom I loved very much.

What do you think your dream means?

I don't know. That's why I am here.

I think you do know. What does this person raping you symbolize to you?

I have no idea, I said and hoped he wouldn't paraphrase Sigmund Freud and all his Oedipal complex and wish-fulfillment theory. Instead, he used Jung as a reference. He stated that dreams have universal symbols. They represent our fears and half-finished thoughts.

When we're awake, we're under control and avoid any extra disturbances if we can avoid them. Dreams grant us the picture of specific situations and state of mind. Your being raped by a loved one, and I can only speculate here, may be the symbol of, I don't know, this person having been demanding upon you and making you do things against your will.

I listened to his explanation with fascination. I was awed by the concept of symbolism. My head was taken with the idea of mastering the science of psychology as soon as time allowed. As the doctor defined the meaning of my dreams, my brain hungered to lay its insatiate fingers on everything there was to know about dreams. Till then, I decided to extract information from the counseling book that sat before me.

What was the other dream?

I once dreamed I was in a place that looked like a mosque. There were lots of people. We were all sitting. Somewhat, the scene resembled the way I imagined the scene in the Bible where Jesus fed his five thousand followers with only two fish and five loaves. This time, though, it seemed that the entire population on Earth was present. At some point, the majestic figure of God hovering above me tapped on my shoulder and, when I looked at Him, He told me that nothing I did was good enough. He said that I had to push myself a lot more and work harder on the things I wanted to accomplish. The day after I dreamed it, I told a friend of mine about it, and she told me that in the dream I had projected my own self in the form of God to tell myself that I wasn't trying hard enough. She said that since I saw God as an almighty being and somehow feared Him, it was ideal to have Him tell me to push myself harder.

I think your friend's interpretation of the dream was right. Dreams reveal a lot about ourselves. You should examine them carefully. Like I told you, make sure you keep a scratch paper and a pen beside your bed, and the moment you wake up, write down anything you remember from the dream you just had.

I nodded, knowing that I'd never follow his instructions. Being brainwashed with a series of clichés in order to solve the puzzles of a very individual head was bad enough, but giving a stranger complete access to my sphere of sleep was out of the question.

Jazz

New York, New York. What verses could I write about you? That you took my breath away. That you left me wanting for more. My mouth has been watering for you ever since my feet landed on your streets. What verses could I write about you? That you're so beautiful I wish I had you here with me. That you're so rich I wish I owned you or you me. So rich of colors and sounds and words. The Spanish young man whom I met at the hostel wondered aloud why I was taking him to all the worst areas. I explained to him how the savor of the world accumulated at the bottom. Like the sugar at the bottom of the glass of a sweet beverage. The kept secret of society. And we strolled on the wide streets of Harlem. Ate burgers and fries in the Bronx. Walked by the water under the bridge in Brooklyn. I couldn't get enough of the bridge. My new friend thought my enthusiasm was out of place. And he couldn't believe his eyes when eventually the subway landed us in Queens. *Finally, a rich neighborhood,* he said. But I wasn't crazy about the orderliness of the area. I liked imperfections because I could toy with them, dress them with stories of my own, or inquire about the history beyond the broken window. And I was fascinated with the people who had borne crosses for centuries. The African Americans who were sold down the river, shipped overseas, and kept captive by the slaveholders. The Native Americans and their bowing backs under the Europeans. The Irish and their oppression for hundreds of years under the English. How could my heart not long to pay reverence to a people whose ancestors bled, were betrayed, humiliated, and sacrificed in their fight for survival? So I longed for more of Harlem. The young English woman whom I took along on my second visit to Harlem said that her mission was to find a white person in that crowd of black faces. She said she was glad I was with her because, with her blond hair and sky-blue eyes, she felt like a souvenir. We spotted white people in the crowd, and the atmosphere became even tastier. So rich of flavors, oh, New York! Little Italy, where Italian was shouted across the green-white-red-banner-covered sky. And Chinatown, where Mandarin and Cantonese were blasted throughout the stores and along the sidewalks. And Times Square, where people spoke Cushitic, Indo-European, Semitic, and Sino-Tibetan languages and more; where the Spanish friend of mine asked me if he could kiss me as we watched *Autumn in New York* and I had to walk out of the movie theater after declining his request. I sat for hours in the middle of Times Square and witnessed the ebb and flow of the throng, and a homeless man's desperate search for food in the trashcan across from me. A passerby offered the homeless man her sandwich, and he sat on the floor, made the sign of the cross, and ate. A stranger joined me in my front-row seat to the best show of wonder and told me the tricks street performers played to make money. Then, he reprimanded a man on a wheelchair for drinking alcohol out in the open like that with the cops around. The man on the wheelchair told him to mind his fucking business. The stranger told me that one is better off helping himself in this crazy city. You open your mouth to help someone else and what do you get? A fucking attitude and a rude remark. And he volunteered information on how the cops had given him a ticket for drinking a beer without a paper bag to cover the bottle. He said he supposed cops didn't want children to see you ain't drinking orange juice. And he went ahead to tell me the number of the street where things were sold very cheap, since they were stolen. By the way, that was the same street where he used to buy his drugs when he used to depend on them, he said. But not anymore. He was clean like crystalline.

I was staying in a youth hostel in East Harlem where you woke up at the sound of Latin music. *Listen to this! I feel like I'm in Venezuela,* said one of the German guests. We sat outside and listened to the rhythm of the night as young people spoke German, Dutch, French, Spanish, and broken English. And I wrote as the guy from Spain recited from memory a poem by Neruda for me. A German medical student said, *What do you write, what do you write, Meti, that yourself is going to be a short story in this crazy city.* And we all laughed. We went to an Irish pub where we watched Tiger Woods play and lose at golf. And we talked about Ireland and books by Oscar Wilde and James Joyce. A crime was announced on the news. It happened somewhere near Queens. One of the boys from Germany said that he was never going to set foot there. A girl from Philadelphia laughed and said how ironic of him to say that when he was practically living and having a drink at one o'clock in the morning in East Harlem. When we got back to the hostel, the German future doctor read my new short story and screamed when he got to the part where the protagonist was reminiscing about having sex on the kitchen table. My English friend asked what the fuss was about. The German asked her how old she was. Nineteen. He told her to cover her ears because Meti wrote too wild a thing and it was no good for young people like her to hear.

I lay across a bench facing the top of the Twin Towers as my Spanish friend sat on the edge of the bench and for the first time I heard him compliment the city of New York. He said that the World Trade Center was the only beauty that he had found in that outrageous city to which I seemed to be losing my heart.

What about the Brooklyn . . .

If you mention that bridge one more time, Meti, I swear I will die.

But it's so beautiful.

But you see beauty even in the garbage. If you want to talk about true beauty, look at that, he said pointing at the Twin Towers.

El cristal. . . .

What does it mean?

How do you Mexicans call it? he said, pointing at the glass windows.

El vidrio, I think, I'm not sure. And I'm not Mexican.

But you speak like them. If you really want to speak Spanish, you should re-learn the language properly. No more encendedor, carro, parqueo, que es eso, tía? Que hables español, no spanglish!

The rain started sprinkling, and my travel buddy complained how tiring it was to be a tourist. And he told me about his betrothed in Spain. I asked him if he was happy, but he shrugged his shoulder.

I don't get enthusiastic over stuff like you do.

But this is your engagement. It's not just the Brooklyn Bridge.

What's the big deal? I'm more scared than happy.

Then, why are you doing it if it doesn't make you happy?

Because I have no choice. I mean, it's inevitable. You meet someone, you date her for years, and then she gives you an ultimatum that you either marry her or she will leave.

You're telling me that you're forced into this engagement?

No, of course not. But it's expected of me sooner or later to get married and settle a family and this looks like it's time. Yet, that doesn't mean that I'm going to go around glowing like you do whenever you see some crazy man dancing with a mannequin in the subway or a group of weirdos singing a cappella in the train and let's not talk about the bridge. I don't know which planet you're from, Meti, cuz it's certainly not Earth, but people of this planet lead a different life from yours and we're what out here we call normal and normal people have to think of marriage and family and kids and don't lose their heart to a city and her crazy ways.

From the dream-world discussion we had had at our previous meeting, I leaped to the unfair reality of my love life. But, first, Dr. Brillantini began with our routine.

Wow, is that a dictionary?

No, it's a book.

It is?

Ahah! The unabridged work of Shakespeare.

Shakespeare, eh? Do you understand the language?

Yeah.

That's amazing. Let me see it. This is a thick book, said Dr. Brillantini as he scanned the names of the plays listed on the back of the book. He twitched his face in an expression of surprise and handed me back the book.

Are you reading it for an English class?

No, just for pleasure.

Shakespeare for pleasure. That's quite phenomenal.

I raised my eyebrow, flattered.

So last time we talked about dreams. What did you get out of our meeting?

I found it interesting when you said that dreams were metaphors revealing our hidden or half-finished thoughts.

Good. What do you want to talk about, today?

Relationships. Men, specifically.

OK. If I remember well, you said you were not dating by choice.

Well, I don't know whether it's a choice. I just can't seem to find the ideal man. And when I like someone, the moment I get his attention I lose interest.

Do you think it may be a defense mechanism? That you run away when you get closer to someone?

Maybe.

What are you afraid of, Meti? asked Dr. Brillantini with such a serious look and voice that it made me question the seriousness of my fears.

I don't know, I answered. *I guess I am afraid of being disappointed. But then again, I do want to fall in love. I think if I meet someone I really like and whose company I really enjoy, I will stick to it. The truth is that it's really hard to find that right someone.*

Meti, you have to know that compromising is a very important thing in the process of building a relationship. Nobody is perfect. There is no such thing as ideal man. You'll have to compromise with the things you don't like in somebody.

I know, but it's so hard. Sometimes I seem to really like someone and have the certainty that we would be perfect together, but he doesn't return my liking.

Do you think that perhaps your permanence in liking those guys has to do with the fact that they don't like you back? That what you really like is the challenge and not the person?

Maybe.

Do you like anyone?

Not exactly. I was after a guy for about fifteen minutes. Literally after him. I'm talking about running from Vine to Highland, down Hollywood Boulevard, screaming his name. When he finally noticed me and stopped, I told him I was interested and I wanted to hang out with him. He said sure, to call him. I went home happy. There was a little earthquake that night but all I could think of was him and our happy life in New York.

New York?

Yeah. He doesn't even like New York. He said it was too fast and crowded. He wanted to move to San Diego, eventually. He also wanted to be an actor. But then again, everybody wants to be an actor in Hollywood.

That means he wasn't just a stranger you ran after. You knew him.

Kinda. He lives in Hollywood so I rode the Fairfax bus to Hollywood to meet up with him and talked for a bit a few minutes before I ran through the crowd and declared myself. I've seen him around for years though. But before, we only said hi to each other.

Did you call?

Oh, yeah. Paged him. Left a message on his machine. Glenn Close straight through. He never called back.

Were you hurt?

For about fifteen minutes. I was mostly mad cuz he'd cost me my earthquake time.

Earthquake time?

I told you there was a little earthquake the day I ran after him but I was too busy thinking about him and didn't enjoy fully the miracle of the earth moving. I love earthquakes.

Very strange. Usually, people are scared of earthquakes.

That too. But it's exciting to lie on the ground and feel the earth move underneath you, watch the furniture shake in the room. It reminds me how small I am, how small man is, how evanescent life is. I did lie on the ground to experience the natural phenomenon that night but, instead of feeling the world around me, I was inventing a world with a man who didn't really exist for me. He didn't even respond to my calls. I missed out on the thrill and the teachings of an earthquake for a man who didn't even have the courage to say he wasn't interested when I told him I was. I hate cowards.

Would you have preferred he told you straight out he wasn't interested?

Of course. The reason I am straightforward with men is that I don't like wasting my time. What's the point of me saying anything to save time if they

*gonna waste it for me with their beating around the bushes? This last one even
wasted my earthquake time.*

Are you always explicit about your feelings?

*They're not feelings. They're moments of window-shopping for an outfit that
pleases the eye before you go into the store to see if it fits and take it home. The
best part of this shopping is that it leads the men to think that they're God-sent
gift to women. Which woman in her right mind would run after a man she
barely knows? I know I'm crazy. And yeah, if I like a guy, he's going to learn it
from me and my very clear words. But this is only temporary. I'm already getting tired of it. I think I'm gonna have to stop running after men who mean
nothing to me.*

*I think you have a threshold when it comes to relationships. You allow your-
self only to that marked point. You are ever careful not to pass it or let someone
else enter it.*

You bet I want to claim my territory, I thought. And perhaps I am not
ready for a relationship or to have someone read my mind, I concluded in
my own head.

Bellydance

Women on my right side. Women on my left side. Women at my feet.
Sarah's large bed was dressed in satin and crushed by the voluptuous bodies of six older women and me. The seven Graces. *The Philosopher Crushed
by Cosmos. Salvador Dali.* Bed the Philosopher. It's all a matter of repre-
sentation. Repose. Sleep. Sex. *SEX?* That is the question.

Sarah, do you know Esu? In Italian.

Yes. Why? You like him? In Amharic.

Well. . . .

And I told the story. About the confusing night. Me and Esu. Sofabed the
Subphilosopher. The clean kisses. The filthy fingers. . . .

Wait, wait a second! Don't tell me you're still. . . .

Wide Large Black Eyes Staring.

Meti! What are you waiting for? How old are you? Twenty?

Twenty-one.

Twenty-one and still a virgin?

Leave me alone!

*Meti, you don't understand. The longer you wait, the harder the hymen will
get and the more it'll hurt when you finally have sex.*

Wide Large Black Eyes Staring.

What's your problem? You haven't lived until you had sex.

I don't have a problem. I'm just not ready. And, honestly, I don't see what's so great about having someone suck your nipples. It hurts like hell. I don't ever want to experience what I went through the other night. And the worst part is that I tried to convince myself that it was OK to be there when I knew very well that the only feeling I had about the moment was to vomit.

You see what you've become for using too much of those brains of yours.

This has nothing to do with my brain. Or maybe, yes. Sex is such a reckless act with life-changing consequences such as emotional attachment, possible pregnancy and diseases. I got too much to lose.

Brains, brains, brains.

The six Graces lectured me for the rest of the night on the importance of separating love from sex. They said that I was the same young girl who had left Rome over four years ago. Not changed a bit. Still hanging out with the dead. But it's time to move on. To step out of this head of mine. To live life.

The next morning I went to visit the Sistine Chapel with Daria. I stood and stared at the ceiling until I grew dizzy. It was *Jubileo* season in Italy. Daria and I befriended two *carabinieri* at the Vatican. *An'vedi questa, parla piú Romano che io!* said one of them in reaction to my fluency in the Roman dialect. We waited on the long line to walk under the sacred door and consequently be absolved of our sins. But my friend told me that I had to make three more stops, *Santa Maria Maggiore, San Giovanni,* and *San Paolo,* if I was aiming for purity. But what was the use? I was in deep shit with the Church.

After the Sistine Chapel and the Vatican visit, I met up with Bela and two friends of hers. We hopped on the train to Florence. I told Bela all about the night with Esu. She was very proud of me. The reassurances were pouring. Didn't matter that I didn't go all the way. Didn't matter that I didn't perform the job on him. Didn't matter that I lay on the sofabed, the subphilosopher, in paralysis, or that I was repelled by it all. And the bastard wasn't surely a noble man. The hell with the bastard. Never gonna see him again, anyway. What mattered was that I embraced the experience. It was time I let myself go. Or at least tried to. Still need work. This feeling-no-pleasure business. This not living in the moment.

That was the end of it. The exploration opened its curtains. (*The red coral of your lips haunts me always and everywhere.*) *The Backbend* on the bed the philosopher Let the body loose Feel not the mattress beneath Regard not the thoughts before you Let go higher and higher Rise to the ceiling and past Reach the skies (*Reducing me to a marigold of wet thoughts*) Move on to *The Belly Roll.* Contract and relax up and down up and down (*Sultry with the heat of your body my being takes the shape of fluid lavishing sumptuously like a hot spring*) *The Figure Eight* Remember no bed the philosopher beneath Paint the number against the empty space around you (*I only seek refuge in your skin, jazzy with jauntiness, silky with delicateness*) Now go on to *The Shimmies* forward and backward forward and backward (*And I thirst for the warmth of your touch, for your hands and solely your hands crusading across the oceans and shores of my body*) Turn and Turn and Turn Now Try the arm ripple can't do it can't go there too dirty too something Dances always best in whole figures Isolations too tricky too daring too difficult too intimate (*This shiver is the realization that you're a mere dream which transformation to reality would take the length of years perhaps centuries Meanwhile the pursuit continues and I can see you and feel you and again my being melts*) A dance without handworks is still a dance.

After two months' time.

The receptionist seemed to be happy to see me. I read the "I knew you would be back" look on his face.

Am I late? I asked right before I looked at the clock that was nailed to the wall beside his desk. It was 12:29. I was one minute early.

Just sign your name and have a seat, he said, going over to the side to get my file.

I stared at him suspiciously. I was sure that he had read the hypothesis written by Dr. Brillantini, who hadn't had the decency to keep it locked somewhere safe. This perfect stranger knows everything that I have told my therapist, I thought to myself. I became uneasy, and, in my head, I scolded the guy who sat behind the desk for his indiscretion.

Hello, there! How are you? Dr. Brillantini interrupted my train of thought.

Fine. How are you?

Great. It's been a while, he said, shaking my hand and opening the healing room door for me.

Bongiorno, he continued, practicing his Italian, this time smiling his non-doctor smile. I only smiled in response. I was bored by these formalities and pleasantries. Then, I thought that to mention my trip in Italy would be relevant to his "Bongiorno!"

I was just there. In Italy.

Really?

Yeah, really.

For how long?

Twenty days.

Wow. How was it? Did you enjoy yourself?

Very much.

Where were you?

In Rome. I also went to Florence for a couple of days. But I was mostly in Rome.

That's great. Did you just get your hair done, or you had it when you went to Rome?

Yeah, I did.

What did they say?

Nothing, really. Except, everyone was looking at me. You know, it's Rome, the founding land of Catholicism. But I think I attracted attention mostly because there are many old people there and I am not so sure they approved of it.

I see. What did your friends say?

They had no comment. I suppose they expected it of me.

They didn't say anything at all?

Blue.

Well, I like it. I think it's beautiful.

Thank you!

So, where do we go from here?

Well, I realized that all the things I used to believe in weren't really my own beliefs. I realized that I don't really have any conviction of my own. The body of beliefs that I've built for years, it's shattered. I am lost. I am convinced of nothing.

OK. Give me some insight.

Well, I lived my entire life being a Catholic, and I don't know anymore what it is to be a Catholic and why am I a Catholic. Or the Church. I don't know anything about it, I mean, about me being in it. I feel as though I borrowed all my convictions and beliefs from other people and society and books. It seems to me now that whatever I said I believed in, it was because it sounded cute.

It was acceptable by people. It was the nice thing to say.

Exactly.

I see your point. He took a look at my file.

You just turned twenty-one.

Yes.

Congratulations! He shook my hand.

Thanks!

We'll return to your speech in a minute. But now, let me ask you something. How do you feel about turning twenty-one? Has there been any change or big event?

No. Not at all.

Did you celebrate it?

No. It was during finals week. I had to study. Plus, no one really remembered it. Except my friend Bela, who called me from Italy and wished me happy birthday on my answering machine. She always remembers my birthday. The only out-of-ordinary thing that I did was on the eleventh, the day before. I went to the Coliseum to see the Virgin Guadalupe whose painting was brought to L.A. from Mexico. I wanted to remind myself that I was born on the same day and month she had appeared to Juan centuries ago. I tried to feel special that way.

He nodded in response.

Well, Meti, I think that whatever is happening with you now has to do with you turning twenty-one. You see, each time our age grows chronologically, we tend to deal with a whole new set of things. Though our psychological maturity develops more rapidly than the chronological order of our age, the age number has an impact on our lives. Have you been feeling the things you mentioned earlier before you turned twenty-one?

Kind of. But now more intensely. I've to admit that I grew very self-conscious about something when I turned twenty-one.

What is it?

I was already twenty-one and I hadn't accomplished much. I haven't published anything.

He smiled his all-knowing smile.

I smiled because I think what you said about not having accomplished much is interesting. You see, among my patients, people your age, I've never had anyone tell me he feels he hasn't accomplished anything in his twenty-one years of life. And I think the fact that you want to contribute to the world so earnestly is great. I think your level of thinking is above the average of people your age. You're ahead of your time. You read a lot. Last time you were here, you were reading Shakespeare for pleasure. Not many people read Shakespeare for the very fact that the language, the old English, is difficult and they are intimidated by it. And you've traveled a lot. You speak many languages. You're curious, so you're constantly learning. You're deep. You have to be more tolerant of yourself. You have to be careful about being intolerant of yourself. You don't want to become your worst critic.

That day, Dr. Brillantini drew a pyramid on the same paper where he had written his hypothesis, to show me the different levels of academic growth. He told me that at eighteen, we're at the bottom of the pyramid, and as we climb up the ladder our minds grow further. He drew small arrows, pointing up for every two or three years of a student's life and related each arrow to the achievement of an A.A., B.A., M.A., and Ph.D. He said that a few years from now I would have a different perspective on life, sex, God, love, relationships, and so on.

I nodded, feigning easiness.

Jarabe Tapatio

The sound of the waves. The presence of sea natives in the breeze. The smell of tobacco on my skin. The taste of tequila on my tongue. The songs of *rancheras* in my head. The dances of Indian warriors and the Spaniards. And I danced in the name of the Aztecs and the Maya. In the name of those who belong to the past. Yet they never left. The marks on their backs and the bloodstains are still present in history. Their songs have been reproduced generation after generation. And I was fortunate enough to be present among a people whose forefathers were conquerors, victims, and warriors. A people who spoke the language of a conqueror, carried the spirit of a warrior, and inherited the humble nature of a victim. México, México, México. I have been possessed, ensnared, bewitched by you.

> *México lindo e querido,*
> *Si muero lejos de ti,*
> *Que digan que estoy dormido*
> *Y que me traigan aquí . . .*

Who is that girl in *traje de luz*? The Matador. Without the bull She is nothing. Someone else's girl. Someone else's future wife. Someone else's daughter. Someone else's friend. Someone else's object of desire or mockery. Someone else's point of reference. The night is inviting. The music is intoxicating. Mariachi. Use all the possible chords in the throat. Going to lose the voice anyhow. All the tequila and Dos Equis will drown the words into whispers.

> *Ay, ay, ay, ay,*
> *Canta y no llores,*
> *Porque cantando se alegran,*
> *Cielito lindo, los corazones.*

Without the crowd she is nothing. Whom would she dress for? Dedicate the round shape of her breasts mirroring through the tight blouse? The nipples bursting through the white laces: two rings of aesthetical proportion. More tequila. More music. The kidnapping. The kerchief covering the mouth. Shshsh . . . !!! My mouth is a funnel. A cone-shaped utensil. My throat is a tube. A hollow passageway to pour *el Presidente* into the small opening of my sober body. Drrruuuuuuuuuuu. . . . Smooth. Swept away off my chair. Swirling. Swirling. Swirling. Round and round. Blurry. Who are you, my prince? I wish to be in your arms like this twirling for the rest of my life. The landing. The body loses its inhibitions to the volatile moment. Rises and falls like the eruption from a volcano. Dance around the imaginary hat. Shall I pick it up in acceptance of the crowd as my eternal partner or keep on dancing? Keep on seducing. . . .

Meti, all signs indicate that our trip is not meant to be, said Blanca in her attempt to dissuade me from my obsessive idea to see La Bufadora, the natural phenomenon not very far from Ensenada, Baja California. I was in Mexico because a friend who worked at the museum back in L.A. had encouraged me to visit her family and although I had never met them before I felt like one of the sisters the moment I got there.

The mugging by the ATM machine, the car crash in Tijuana involving the young man we had met at Hussong's just a week ago. . . . Something bad was gonna happen.

Nothing bad is gonna happen.

The reason Blanca, her sister Cristina, their cousin, and Cristina's boyfriend, Pinocchio, were reluctant about the trip was the road. It was curvy and deadly. They were parking the car at a gas station and I asked how was beer going to help make the road less dangerous. Who said anything about getting beer? They were going to buy fuel for the engine. Blanca and Pinocchio came back with a few six-packs.

Cerveza è combustible por el carro?

Yes, Nefertiti, it was fuel for the car that ran down the stomach. I was really beginning to believe that drinking beer was obligatory while driving in Mexico, as wearing a seatbelt was in California. The day after I arrived in Ensenada, Blanca and her friend insisted that I sit in the front of the car with them with no seatbelt and no seat for that matter as we drove to the beach, drinking Dos Equis and singing *rancheras* and songs by Mana and Ricardo Arjona.

No drinking in the car. Especially, you, Pinocchio!

But Nefertiti, they had to. They had to forget that I was making them venture off on a suicide trip. If something bad was going to happen, it wasn't certainly because of Dos Equis and Tecate. They had told me about the signs, but I wouldn't listen. And I said that if the driver was going to drive drinking, then I might as well say goodbye to the world properly, so I opened a beer bottle with my teeth and cheered our death.

Now, we're talking, Nefertiti.

We arrived at La Bufadora safe and tipsy. The phenomenon was magnificent and worthy of its fame. And fame was also my name when street vendors recognized me as the girl who had danced on top of a platform next to the stage at a club in Ensenada.

Hey, you're the dancer!

A street vendor dared me to eat a live worm.

I've eaten a fried one before.

This is much tastier.

My friends said that if I ate that worm, they would see me no longer as Meti the Nefertiti but as Meti the worm-eater.

You eat it first.

He did.

Let me see how it tastes.

He dispensed a new worm onto my tongue like the Eucharist. I licked it and handed it back to him, shaking my head. When I walked back to the car, Pinocchio had bought more Dos Equis and said that since we weren't driving, it was a good time to drink. How did he think we were getting back into town? Flying? No, the six-packs would sober up in a few minutes. Plus, on the way back we'd be on the other side of the road. The people driving the opposite way would have to go down the hill first and be our cushions when we crashed. I grabbed a beer and Pinocchio shared his Cuban cigar with me. By the time we were back on the road, we were as intoxicated as we could get and I was in heaven from smoking the cigar.

Dr. Brillantini asked what was I reading as usual.

The Waves *by Virginia Woolf.*

How do you like it?

Oh, I love it.

What is it about?

It narrates the lives of six people from childhood to their adult years. It's cool because the author reveals the characters by presenting their stream of thought as opposed to what goes on outside them, I said enthusiastically.

Interesting, he said. *I am glad you're enjoying it. So?*

I saw a movie called Sex, Lies, *and* Videotape *last night. The title was a perfect metaphor for my life.*

How so?

Sex represents the taboo world I lived in my entire life and all the things that I have been forbidden to have, to speak, to think. Lies are the cover-up for having dared to eat the fruit, and the videotapes symbolize the final moment of revelation. The confession.

The confession?

My writing. If I didn't write, I don't know what would have become of me. The blank pages inspire my confidence. I don't trust people. No one. But those blank pages. . . . I could marry into a family of blank paper.

A long pause.

The truth has been presented to me as a very scary thing ever since I can't remember. It's never been, 'Meti, speak up!' It's always been, 'Meti, keep quiet!' 'Don't tell them who where or what you've been.' It's so tiring to lie, to hide the past, to be ashamed of who you are.

Are you ashamed of who you are?

I used to be.

What were you ashamed of?

Being from Ethiopia. Being black. Being familyless.

What is so shameful about those things?

The history.

The history?

Yes, the history. The reputation that being from Ethiopia or the other things have. Everywhere I go, people are asking me whether the images of the starving children on TV are real. They ask me if I ever wished to be white. And you know what I do? I lie. I tell them there's no starving children in Ethiopia, at least not where I lived, and that I never wished to be white. But the problem is not just Ethiopia or my skin. Just about everything. I project an image that is not me. I put on a mask and walk around assuming the role of someone who's foreign even to myself. Sometimes, I can't even recognize myself.

I think the problem is that you're comfortable in this role you play. You're used to it. You need what an alcoholic needs to stay sober. Discipline. You need to train yourself to be true to yourself. You need to maintain yourself sober. People will never know you if you don't tell them who you are.

A short pause.

Next time, I want us to try age regression.

What's that?

It's a method used in therapy to recall forgotten events from the past.
Hypnosis?
Not quite.
What did you say it's called?
I don't want you to go and look it up.

Tango

Here they come!
Who?
Los balseros.
Where?
You see the lights far into the ocean? Ves las balsas?
They must be the border patrol officers.
No, Meti, the Cubans. They travel at night, and when they reach land, they
run to the Estefans' club to dry themselves.
The one downtown?
No, the one in South Beach.
But that's right here, behind us.
Right. Can't you see them coming in this direction? If we stick around long
enough, we may even meet them. Would you like to meet the Cubans, Meti?
A la chingada con ustedes! I actually believed you for a moment.

It was a lovely summer night in South Beach, Miami. The storytellers were
a woman from Panama and two men from Argentina, all of whom I had
met at the hostel where I was staying. We were sitting on the sand by the
shore, drinking Argentine mate and playing with Meti's head. The hostel
was two blocks from the beach, and if we weren't outside the hostel drinking either sangria or mate and listening to stories that belonged to distant
lands, we were on the beach listening to more stories of distant lands and
drinking herb imported from Argentina.

There were two categories of people at the hostel: the tourists like me
and the immigrants who were living in the hostel.

I miss Buenos Aires. I miss my friends. I miss my car.

We were sitting in a circle, and they passed the mate around. It was a ceremony. It was a dance performance. *El circulo* in tango. One and Three.
One and Three. Tan and Go. Tan and Go. The thermos bottle is everybody's leader. It's pivoting to the left after allowing one sip or two per fol-
lower and circling back to the beginning.

Eew. The word slipped from my mouth. The mate was stronger that the mate I had experienced in the past days.

Meti, that is the biggest form of disrespect. Mate is sacred, said the nostalgic young man who longed for his Buenos Aires, his friends, and his car.

Leave her alone. She didn't know. Not everyone's world revolves around Argentina, said Karina in my defense. Karina was the brave crusader from Argentina.

I am sorry if I offended you, I apologized.

But I was grateful to him for scolding me. I was grateful to God for allowing me to be present at that moment, in that circle, with those specific people. Those people were my first experience of Argentina. And they were more expressive and beautiful than the tango I admired reverently. If life was an endless possibility of encounters like those, I welcomed her with open arms.

Quickly Belgium, said Dier, a tourist from Belgium. His comment on the urge to go to Belgium was his reaction to the french fry that he had tasted from my plate.

Quickly to Belgium? we asked in unison, Himmel and I, seeing no relation between the conversation that we were having and Belgium.

The fries taste bad.

And?

In Belgium, we have exquisite fries.

It was his accent that was exquisite. So when I wasn't with the South Americans drinking mate and sangria, I was with the Europeans (from Belgium, France, and Sweden), drinking beer. I grew nostalgic for the places I had never visited. I grew nostalgic for Cuba as I lost my eyes in the distance of the ocean at night and ate pork chops at restaurants in Little Havana and gulped down *mojito cubano* and listened to the old man sitting beside me on the bus tell me stories of once upon a time in Havana. I grew nostalgic for Argentina as I sipped the mate and listened to the tragic tango of economy decadence and changes of heart about presidents. I grew nostalgic for Sweden as I was given access, through my friend's old soul mind, to the rune stones and the chiaroscuro of the capital's beauty, her waterways and cobblestone streets. Himmel was my beach buddy from Sweden. We lay under the sun all day, and while her skin changed to a tannish color, mine became black as coal. The boys drank beer all day, and by night they were completely wasted.

Beer?

No. Dier. Where is he?
You want beer?
No. Dier from Belgium.
No. This is Corona from Mexico.

I didn't look up age regression. I wanted to be surprised. On our next meeting, when I walked in the room, Dr. Brillantini asked for my permission to bring in an M.D.

What does M.D. stand for?
A medical doctor.
What's a medical doctor?
Someone who treats the body as opposed to the mind.
Why does she want to hear my problems?
She wants to see how this is done.
I don't care.

But the moment she walked in, I regretted having granted one more stranger access to my past.

Dr. Brillantini began his magic.

Lie down. Make yourself comfortable. Close your eyes. Relax. Relax your body. Relax your toes. One by one. Relax your feet. Your right foot first. Now your left foot. Relax your heels. Relax your calves. Relax your knees. Relax your thighs. . . .

He asked me to relax every part of my body. Then, he began knocking on the door of my so-called past.

You are two. What do you see?

Nothing, I said and found his question to be derisory. What in the hell was I supposed to remember of the time I was two?

You are three. What do you see?

Nothing.

You are four. What do you see?

Nothing. If this man doesn't get a bit more creative or if this age regression thing doesn't offer more than this what-do-you-see game, I am going to walk out of this room.

You are five. What do you see?

Nothing.

You are six. What do you see?

There is no way I can remember that far. I have some vivid images and some faded ones, but I don't know whether they took place when I was five or nine.

I never placed importance on the chronological growth of my age. I didn't keep track of events in parallel to what age I was. With me, it's never like I was in second or fifth grade when this happened. This happened period.

I knew I had spoiled the plan. The plan was not for me to rant like that. The plan was for me to remember gradually and dramatically, like a picture in slow motion. The plan was for my voice to tremble and for the words to fall out of my memory like broken glasses.

You are seven. What do you see?

There was no use in trying to make him, myself, or anyone else understand that coming to terms with the past could not be so simple. I wanted to scream that his voice uttering the verb "Relax!" wasn't going to bring my body to complete obedience. And who thought of this crazy idea that relaxing would lead to remembering? Moreover, I didn't want to relax. I couldn't afford to relax. What does he or anyone know about my eternal existence in the box ring? I must be tense at all times. I must live with a ready fist and an intent gaze, swinging, protecting my back and front and sides. Relax? What do they think this is? A vacation? I have a fight to attend every minute of the day every day of the week every week of the month every month of the year.

Variation

I walk the lonely streets of this crowded city they call the city of angels, bearing a loaded mind and a heavy heart. My cross isn't the sins of the world. My cross is you. Whoever you are, wherever you are. I am a sponge and I absorb your absence, counting to one hundred and back to zero and once again to a hundred. I am too small for this place, too small for you. I am being swallowed by the immensity of your large hands, by the loud roar of your laughter. The moon shows me sympathy. We cross glances, but then I am reminded how she's dead, lifeless, a mere corpse. I lie underneath the corpse and breathe in the night's air, the darkness, the smell of all intangible things. I've memories of past sensations, and they pierce through my skin, reduce me to a shiver. I close my eyes and let love come to me and wash me. The love of you. The love of her. The love of him. Your being a stranger fills me to the head. I want to keep you there. Whoever you are, wherever you are. I want you to be everything. A possibility of change, of love, of tomorrow, of happiness, of belief. I will gather myself: my thoughts, my fears, my voice will all be of one piece. I will ready my heart for you; fold neatly the garments of forsaken entities; provide a supply of wax to make candles in times of need. I beg you for only one thing: Please, don't show up! Let me wait for eternity. Allow my heart to race endlessly, never running into you but always expecting to see you any minute now. It is here that I want to cease, caught in the middle of a race, on my way to you.